Easy English Stories

Easy English Stories

herausgegeben von
Vera K. G. Dale und Willy Piert

Ernst Klett Verlag

ISBN 3-12-524620-2

2. Auflage 2 57 56 55 54 | 1990 89 88 87

Alle Drucke dieser Auflage können im Unterricht nebeneinander benutzt werden, sie sind untereinander unverändert. Die letzte Zahl bezeichnet das Jahr dieses Druckes.

Druck: Herzogsche Druckerei, Stuttgart. Printed in Germany.

Vorwort

Easy English Stories sind eine Sammlung meist heiterer und spannender Geschichten. Sie sind mit einem ausführlichen Vokabular versehen, damit sie als lehrbuchunabhängige Lektüre vom zweiten Lernjahr an verwendet werden können. Ihr Wortschatz bewegt sich im wesentlichen innerhalb der ersten 2000 Grundwörter. Die Texte sind nach steigender Schwierigkeit geordnet. Thematik und Wortschatz ermöglichen außerdem ihre Verwendung als leichte Nacherzählstoffe.

Die rechts neben den Titeln angegebenen Zahlen verweisen auf die entsprechenden Lektionen des Lehrbuches *Englisch* von Eckermann-Piert (Klettbuch 5046). Auf dem Wortschatz und den grammatischen Strukturen dieser Lektionen bauen die vorliegenden Erzählungen auf. Sie geben aber auch dem Lehrer, der sie neben einem anderen Lehrbuch verwendet, gute Gelegenheit, bestimmte grammatische Erscheinungen in konzentrierter Form zu wiederholen.

Mit dieser Sammlung kommt der Verlag einem aus Lehrerkreisen vielfach geäußerten Wunsch nach zusätzlichen Lesetexten entgegen. Die Verfasser danken Herrn Fachschuloberlehrer Zeno Alberti, Koblenz, für seine wertvollen Anregungen, die zum Zustandekommen der Sammlung führten.

Februar 1978

Inhalt

Vorbemerkung: Die Texte bauen auf den unter *Grammatik* angeführten Stoffen auf. Die in Klammern angegebenen Lektionen beziehen sich auf das Lehrbuch *Englisch* von Eckermann-Piert. Diese Lektionen behandeln die Grammatik und werden durch die Texte dieser Sammlung ergänzt.

1. Christmas Presents

L 12

It is three days before Christmas. Sally, a nice young girl of twenty-one, enters the big store. She wants to buy some presents for her friend Bill. What can she buy? The big store provides everything from a haircut to a honeymoon, if people have the money. But Sally hasn't got much money.

She is dreaming of a white Christmas and she is dreaming of Bill. She wants to buy him a nice present, but all the nice presents are so expensive.

Bill is a detective in the big store. From his office near the entrance he watches the different departments on television.

In the men's department he sees Sally. She looks sweet with her fair hair and slim figure. What is she doing in the men's department? She takes two shirts, then a red tie, a green pullover and blue socks. There's no assistant in the department. Bill gets a big shock. Does Sally forget to pay for all those things? She's leaving the men's department. Bill watches her on television. Can he show Sally to his family? Can he marry her, if she doesn't pay? No, he can't. Bill is very sad.

But what's that? Sally goes to another department and shows the shirts, the pullover, the socks and the tie. Then she pays for all those things on her arm.

Bill is happy. Now he can buy her a nice wedding present, now he can marry her.

On Christmas day Sally takes Bill to the Christmas tree. "Do you know what I have got for you, Bill?"

„Yes, Sally, I do. A green pullover, a red tie, two shirts and blue socks."

2. Grandma Sophia

L 13

A Belgian boat enters Dover Harbour. The passengers are on deck with their luggage. Twenty minutes later an Italian lady, her name is Signora Capone, is going to the customs hall.

"Which of these suitcases is yours?" asks the customs officer.

Signora Capone points to two large cases. No, she has nothing to declare, no presents, no cameras, nothing at all. But she must open her luggage. "What's this?" asks the officer, as he finds one gold watch after the other, ten in all. Then he produces eight silver cigarette-cases. "Will you please come with me?" says the customs officer and takes Signora Capone to the main office. There she has to answer a lot of questions.

Two hours later the Signora is in a train to London. She is not very happy. What presents can she give her family in London? All her silver cigarette-cases and all her watches are at the customs in Dover.

When Signora Capone arrives in London, her son Carlo Capone and his five children welcome her with smiles and kisses. But Carlo sees that there is no smile on his mother's face.

"What makes you so sad, Mother? Aren't you happy to see us again?"

In the taxi Signora Capone tells her son about the customs in Dover.

"Never mind, dear," says Carlo. "Better luck next time. We must get the money back. I've got an idea."

Next day Carlo and Sophia take the train to Brighton with Carlo's five children. On Brighton pier there is a beauty competition for the most attractive grandma.

The grandmas walk with their grandchildren in front of the judges. What chance has Grandma Sophia got? She looks nice in her new Harrods dress and all her little grandchildren behind her. The judges watch the beauty parade.

Signora Capone wins. She is Brighton's most attractive grandma. Miss Lily Pond, the film star, gives out the prizes. What does Signora Capone get? Twenty pounds for each grandchild, a gold watch and a silver cigarette-case.

Next day Grandma Capone's picture is in the newspapers. A hundred copies go to Rome.

3. A Sunday Morning Dream

L 14

Dick and Mary are a young married couple. They have a small flat. In the week Dick is the ideal husband. He does everything for Mary. He brings her a cup of tea in the morning, he has breakfast at her bedside, he washes up the dishes.

But on Sundays Dick always stays in bed until half past eleven. On that day Mary gets up at a quarter to ten and goes to the kitchen where she has a cup of tea. She never has breakfast on Sundays because she is slimming and because Dick is in bed.

When the church clock strikes ten, she switches on the radio. The Sunday morning programme is boring. So Mary fetches the Sunday newspaper from the front door, then goes to the sitting-room and begins to read.

There are many interesting things in the paper. Freddie Dent, the actor, is going to marry Lily Pond, the film star. Harrods, the big store where the Queen often buys presents, is providing the wedding dress, the champagne with waiter, the wedding cake, the flowers. Freddie Dent's wedding present for Lily is going to be a white Rolls Royce.

Mary gets up from her chair and looks in the mirror. Isn't she a beautiful woman, too? Hasn't she got a nice face, a good figure? Don't people look at her when she enters a restaurant in the West End? Why isn't she a film star? Why can't she have a white Rolls Royce? Why isn't she going away to Italy for her holidays? With Dick she always spends her holidays at Brighton, in a cheap guest-house near the station. Every minute they hear the trains. The other guests are boring people like the Smith family.

Mary is dreaming in front of the mirror. She is dreaming of the white Rolls Royce with her and Dick in it. They are driving to their beautiful big house in Wimbledon with nice flowers in the garden. They are going to have a lot of guests in the evening.

At that moment she hears Dick's voice from the bedroom, "Mary, darling, I'm waiting for my breakfast. Sunday is my free day."

4. The Girl Next Door

L 15

The old gentleman in the boat train gave me the address: Warwick Terrace 83 or 38. "It's very central. The landlady is a young widow. You'll be very happy there."

When I arrived at Warwick Terrace I looked for number 83, but there was no such number in the street. There was a number 38. A thin lady with orange-coloured hair welcomed me and showed me a dark room under the roof with a very small window. I did not like the room but I stayed there for three weeks.

Every morning at seven o'clock the thin old landlady with orange-coloured hair entered my room with a cup of tea. Every morning she looked at me and said, "Here's a nice cup of tea for you. It's a nice morning this morning."

At last I decided to leave that awful room under the roof and go to a better place. That morning when I wanted to go the old landlady opened the door of my room and said, "You've got a new neighbour now. A very nice young lady of eighteen. Oh, she's a most attractive girl. She comes from Dover and she is an assistant in a big store."

At once I decided to stay. Days passed, but I didn't see my beautiful neighbour. I waited for her in the morning, I waited for her in the evening. My heart was full of expectation. Was she like Lily Pond, the film star? I wondered what she was like. Was her hair dark or fair? Were her eyes brown or blue? I didn't go out in the evenings because I wanted to meet her. When I heard a noise outside my room, I rushed to the door, but it was always the old landlady. She looked at me with her black eyes and asked with a smile, "What can I do for you?"

One morning the maid opened the door of my room to bring my morning tea. The landlady was ill in bed. She had a bad cold.

"Bring the tea to my neighbour first," I said to the maid.

"Which neighbour?" she asked.

"The young lady next door," I replied.

"There is no young lady next door," answered the maid. "The landlady often writes her letters there. It's her office."

Do I need to tell you that I didn't stay another day at that boarding-house? But I often dream of the landlady with orange-coloured hair. She laughs and shows me a mouse-trap.

5. Aunt Lily's Letter

L 16

Aunt Lily was an old landlady with orange-coloured hair. Her boarding-house was in Warwick Terrace. She had relatives in Wimbledon. Every evening Aunt Lily took the train to Wimbledon to keep them company. Her nephew was alone with the children because his wife was away on holiday. Here is a letter from Aunt Lily to her nephew's wife.

38, Warwick Terrace
London W 2
July 3, 1970

My dear Ann,

On Monday I went to see your family in Wimbledon, but they were not at home. They had all gone to a restaurant, because there was no food in the house. Your daughter Mary had forgotten to go shopping. It was very hot that day and all the windows were open. As I couldn't wait, I went home again. Later your dear husband, Jack, phoned me. The burglars had called and had stolen your beautiful fur coat. It made me very sad.

The house looks awful without you. The sugar is in the tea-pot, there is butter in the marmalade, and the cat has had her kittens in the best armchair in the sitting-room.

By the way, I think Jack drinks too much. On Tuesday his father gave him some rum for his cold. He drank five glasses. Of course, I drank with him so that he couldn't drink it all. Later he phoned for a taxi, because I couldn't walk to the station. I had to pay one pound for the taxi. Jack never gave me that pound back. When I called on Jack the next day, the rum was all gone.

Your family isn't very nice to me. When there's a good film on TV, they always want to watch football. It's so boring. They take no notice when I pull a long face.

Mary hasn't been a very good cook. We've had tinned food for supper every evening. The tinned tomato soup and the potatoes were always cold.

My German boarder has gone. He didn't like his room. Aren't these Germans difficult! Fortunately I have a new boarder for that lovely room under the roof. An Italian lady has got it now. Her name is Signora Capone.

Are you coming back soon? We miss you.

Love from
Aunt Lily

6. Derby Day in Epsom

L 17

"Good afternoon, ladies and gentlemen. This is George Taylor speaking. I'm reporting from the race-course at Epsom. It's a beautiful day. Well over a hundred thousand people are waiting with me for the big race, the Derby. It's five minutes to three, and at three o'clock the race begins for the three-year-old horses.

The Queen and the Royal Family have just arrived. For those without colour television I must say that the Queen is wearing a pink hat, a white dress and pink shoes. She looks beautiful.

Who do I see now, ladies and gentlemen? Freddie Dent, the great actor, and his wife Lily Pond, the film star with the slim figure. Hello, Freddie, hello, Lily. It's nice to see you. Please say a few words to the millions in Britain. They are watching you.

Freddie Dent: Good afternoon, friends. I think your horse has a good chance to win.

G. Taylor: Thank you, Freddie. That's very nice of you. Now it's your turn, Lily.

Lily Pond: Good luck to you all. Back the right horse!

G. Taylor: You're very kind, Lily. Now, Freddie, tell me what's your next film?

Freddie Dent: 'The Ideal Husband'.

G. Taylor: That's very interesting.

Freddie Dent: Lily is playing the ideal wife and I'm the ideal husband.

G. Taylor: In three words—the ideal couple. (They all laugh.) Thank you, Lily, thank you, Freddie. Good-bye and good luck!

Ladies and gentlemen, the horse parade has begun. There are twenty horses on the race-course. It's a beautiful picture. Lovely women, wonderful hats and dresses, ideal horses. They are off! Now they come round the corner. Royal Fly, the Queen's horse, leads the field, a French horse is close behind. Still five hundred yards to go. Royal Fly in front, Dublin, an Irish horse is second, Winterwolf, a German horse is third. The winning-post is in sight. Ladies and gentlemen, a fourth horse shoots to the front like an arrow. Which horse is it? It's Torelli, the Italian horse. It overtakes Winterwolf, it overtakes Dublin, it overtakes the royal colours. Torelli is 80 to 1 Derby winner. Torelli wins 40,000 pounds."

7. Tom and Shirley

L 18

Tom and Shirley Brown are a young married couple. They have a nice house in Bromley. "Home, sweet home," is Tom Brown's motto. He always brings his wife some sweets and hands them to her with the words, "Sweets for the sweet." She always welcomes him with a smile and a kiss. During the week-end there is always something to do for Tom in the garden and in the house. There are the flowers to water, some curtains to hang up or a carpet to nail down. Nothing is too much for him. He is the ideal husband.

One day Tom comes home from the office in the afternoon. When he enters the house Shirley is just dialling a telephone number. Who is she phoning? Tom is listening behind the door of the sitting-room. Three times the number is engaged. The fourth time Shirley gets through.

"British Overseas Airways? This is Mrs Brown speaking. Are there any flights to New York on April 2nd? Will you please reserve two first class seats in the name of Mrs Shirley Brown. What are the times of departure and arrival? Are there any stops on the way? There aren't any? That's fine. I want to travel back on April 16th, so I want two return tickets. Can I also book a hotel room? Yes, a double room with bath in a good hotel for a fortnight. Can I get the tickets in the morning? Thank you."

Tom cannot believe it. Is Shirley going to run away from him? Has he done anything wrong? He is very sad, but an Englishman does not like to show his feelings. That is what Tom learned at school, that is what he practises in later life.

He doesn't want any food for supper. He has some whisky instead.

"Can I do anything for you, darling?" Shirley asks. "Are you ill?"

No, Tom is not ill. Only some trouble at the office. That's all. Tom goes into the garden. The date is March 10th. Shirley is going to leave on April 2nd. Three more weeks ...

Two days later it is Tom's birthday. There's a letter under his cup and saucer. As he opens the envelope two large passenger tickets for a flight to New York are in his hands.

"Happy birthday, darling," says Shirley. "Do you like my present? We are going to spend a fortnight in New York."

"But we haven't got any money for that," says Tom.

"Of course we have, darling. I won £2,000 in the football pools last week. Your holiday begins on April 2nd and so ..."

8. The Future

The shop window was full of notices. A young man stopped and looked at them. One was very interesting:

Mrs Scott, 38 Warwick Terrace, near Paddington Station, will tell you your future.

Five minutes later the young man rang at Mrs Scott's. A thin woman with orange-coloured hair opened the door.

"Come in," she said with a smile.

The young man followed her through the dark hall into a big sitting-room.

"Would you like to sit down," the woman said and pointed to a chair. "What can I do for you?"

"Well," replied the young man. "I saw your interesting notice in the shop-window..."

"Do you want to know your future?" asked the woman. "That'll be two pounds."

The young man handed her the money.

"Now let me see your hand, dear. Yes, the left hand. You'll become a great actor. Your future wife will be an attractive film star. You'll have three daughters, but you won't have any sons. You'll have plenty of money, but I wouldn't put it all on horses. I'd buy some houses."

"Will my future wife have fair hair?" asked the young man.

"Your wife will have dark hair, but don't worry. She'll be very beautiful."

"That's fine," said the young man. "Now would you show me your hand, Mrs Scott?"

"My hand? What for?"

"Well, I'll tell you your future now. You won't have to give me any money, but I think you'll give me back my two pounds when I have finished."

"I won't," cried Mrs Scott.

"I wouldn't be so sure," said the young man. "Let me see your hand."

Mrs Scott gave him her hand.

"Listen, Mrs Scott, you can't tell the future. I am married. My wife has fair hair. I haven't got any daughter but I've got two sons. I won't become an actor. I am a policeman. Your future won't be very bright, if you don't stop this game. Will you give me back my two pounds now?"

Mrs Scott pulled a long face. "Here's your money," she said.

"Thank you," said the young policeman. "We'll watch you in future. Good-bye."

9. A Bet

L 20

England was the country of the Anglo-Saxons. Then, in the year 1066, the Normans conquered England. They spoke French. There were then two languages in the country. That is why today English is a mixture of Germanic and French words.

Every year thousands of young people go to Britain to learn the English language. One evening Miss Vandenberg, an attractive Dutch girl of twenty, and Herr Mosbach, a young Austrian, came out of their evening class. As they stepped into the street, Herr Mosbach spoke to her.

Herr M.: You are Dutch, aren't you, Miss Vandenberg?

Miss V.: Yes, Mr Mosbach, I am. Are you Austrian?

Herr M.: Yes. I'm in England to learn the language.

Miss V.: It's not always easy, is it?

Herr M.: No, it isn't. I wish the Normans hadn't conquered England.

Miss V.: Why, Mr Mosbach?

Herr M.: Then English would be a Germanic language. We wouldn't have to learn so many words of French origin. You and I speak Germanic languages.

Miss V.: That's right. English would be easy for us, wouldn't it?

Herr M.: It would be easy for me, if I could learn it with you. May I learn it with you, Miss Vandenberg?

Miss V.: Well, why not, Herr Mosbach. Where could we learn it together?

Herr M.: I know a nice restaurant not far from here. We needn't take the bus. We could have dinner together, couldn't we? May I ask you to be my guest, Miss Vandenberg?

Miss V.: Thank you, Mr Mosbach. That's very nice of you. Let's have a bet. We'll read the menu. If there are more words for food of Germanic origin, I'll pay for the meal. If there are more words of French origin, you'll pay.

Twenty minutes later Miss Vandenberg and Herr Mosbach enter a small restaurant near Hyde Park.

Waiter: A table for two, sir? There's a nice table here, sir. Would that be all right?

Herr M.: Thank you. (They sit down.) Can we have the menu?

Waiter: Yes, sir. Here it is. (He hands the menu to Miss Vandenberg. Herr Mosbach and Miss Vandenberg sit side by side and look at it together.)

Herr M.: Shall we begin with some soup?

Miss V.: Tomato soup for me, please. Soup is of French origin. It's *la soupe* in French. One point for me.

Herr M.: We'll have bread and butter. Bread and butter are Germanic words. Two points for me.

Miss V.: For meat there's veal, beef and mutton. Meat, veal, beef and mutton are of French origin. Four more points for me. I've got five points in all now. I'll have a beefsteak.

Herr M.: I'll have a steak, too. But steak is Germanic. It has the same origin as the German word *Stück*. Three points for me.

Miss V.: Now let's look at the vegetables. I'll have green peas. Vegetables and peas are of French origin. Seven points for me.

Herr M.: And I'll have beans. The German word is *Bohne*. Four points for me.

Miss V.: I'll have some fruit. Fruit is French. Eight points for me.

Herr M.: And I'll have cheese and biscuits. And later a sweet with a lot of milk. Cheese, sweet and milk are of Germanic origin. Seven points for me.

Miss V.: You've forgotten the biscuits. Biscuit is a French word. Nine points for me. You have seven. I've won our bet.

Waiter: Excuse me, madam. This is not correct. I'm a student of languages. If I may say so the word 'soup' is not of French but of Germanic origin. Its origin is *Suff*. Would you like something to drink?

10. Fast Cars

During the week Ingrid Müller, a German girl of twenty-two, was a companion to an invalid old lady. At week-ends she was free. On those days she often went to the cinema, to a dance or to the seaside.

One Saturday afternoon Ingrid stood at the bus stop. She wanted to go to the tennis international at Wimbledon. Suddenly a young man in a beautiful red car stopped in front of Ingrid.

"Are you waiting for a bus?" he asked with a winning smile. "They don't run very often on Saturdays. Can I help you?"

"I want to see the tennis international at Wimbledon," said Ingrid quickly.

"That's on my way," said the young man. "Get in. I'll take you there."

Ingrid accepted gladly.

"You're a foreigner, aren't you?" asked the young man as the car started again.

"I'm German," replied Ingrid. "I'm here to learn English."

Ingrid looked at the young man. He was tall and dark. Where had she seen that face before? Suddenly she remembered. They had shown his face the evening before on television in *Help the Police*. The man was a burglar. He had been in prison and had run away. The beautiful red car was stolen. What could Ingrid do? Jump out of the car at the next traffic lights? The traffic lights were green all the time. Ingrid was terribly miserable. Suddenly she got an idea.

"Your car doesn't run very fast, does it?" she said to the young man. "You should see our German cars. They're awfully quick, even the Volkswagen."

That was too much for the young man.

"You don't know what a British car can do," he said. "Just watch."

Like an arrow the car shot through the streets and overtook all the other cars on the road.

"It's lovely!" Ingrid gave a shout of pleasure. "It's lovely! I like fast cars. You drive very well."

The stranger smiled happily.

"Yes," he said. "Look, 120 miles. That's what a British car can do."

Suddenly a police car was behind them. The young man saw it in his driving-mirror. "The pigs," he said. "But they won't get me."

He raced round the corners, took no notice of the red traffic lights, and did his best to get away. But his best did not help him. The police were still behind them like dogs behind a cat. Then the police car easily overtook the red car and stopped it. The policemen took Ingrid and the young man to the police station. They first thought that she was the burglar's girl-friend. They phoned the invalid old lady, and she told the police that Ingrid was her companion. A police car took the stranger back to prison while Ingrid took a taxi to the tennis international at Wimbledon.

11. A Second-hand Car L 22

Good car to sell. £5. Apply 29, Greenleaf Rd, E. 17.

When Bill saw this advertisement in the newspaper, he decided not to go to his office that morning. He took the tube to Greenleaf Road instead. He looked for number 29. He knocked, waited and a woman of about forty opened the door.

"I saw your advertisement in the paper," Bill said. "Can I see the car?"

"Yes," said the woman. "It's in the garage. The door is open. Just go and have a look at it."

Bill went to the garage and opened it. There he saw a car. It was red and it was new.

Bill went back to the front door again.

"I wanted to buy a car for five pounds," he said. "That car in the garage is practically new."

"That's all right," said the woman. "You can have that car for five pounds. You see my husband left me and ran away to New York. He'll never come back. In a letter he told me to sell the car and to send him the money. Well, I'm selling it for five pounds."

Bill gave the woman the five pounds and took the car. Then he drove to his friend Marjorie.

"Get in, Marjorie," he said. "We are going for a drive. This beauty belongs to me. I didn't steal it. I bought it for five pounds."

Bill pressed the starter, put the car into bottom gear, and off they went. A few minutes later they had left the town behind them. While the car was speeding along a narrow country road, Bill looked at the speedometer. The needle was pointing to 70 miles. Marjorie and Bill were enjoying their drive when the car suddenly slowed down and then stopped. Several times Bill tried the starter, but the engine didn't run. He climbed out and lifted the bonnet. He turned a few screws. But still the engine would not start.

"That woman played me a trick this morning," said Bill to Marjorie as they were pushing the car along the road to the nearest garage three miles away. "I knew something was wrong. That car isn't worth five pounds. Two pounds is too much for it."

At the garage the mechanic glanced at the engine, looked at the petrol and said to Bill, "How many gallons, sir? The tank is empty. Filling-station outside."

12. The Superstitious Football Player — L 23

Charlie Webber was one of the best football players in England. With him his club won most of their matches. People called him 'Charlie the Bomber'.

Nobody could be more superstitious than Charlie. When he saw a black cat in the street, he turned round and went home again. He always wore a lucky charm round his neck, a little pig. He never played football on a Friday, he never walked under a ladder. Once he met a very nice girl. He liked her and she liked him. When she told him the date of her birth, he left her. Her birthday was on the thirteenth.

The great event on the football field had come: the match England versus Italy. As the match was going to start at 3 o'clock, Charlie Webber left his home an hour before. In the car he got a big shock. He had left his lucky charm in the bathroom. It was too late to go back and fetch it. Three miles further on, the car suddenly slowed down and stopped. The petrol tank was empty. He had to leave the car on the road, but reached Wembley in good time for the match. In the dressing-room some players were playing with a football. As the ball came to Charlie, he kicked it against a mirror. The mirror broke to pieces. Charlie turned as white as a sheet.

"Seven years bad luck," he thought.

More than 100,000 spectators were round the football field. They had come to see England win, for England was the great favourite. When the match began, their hearts were full of expectation. There were shouts of excitement as Charlie suddenly stood with the ball in front of the Italian goal. But Charlie fell and an Italian player kicked the ball back into the field. Everything went wrong for Charlie on that day. He was the worst of the 22 players, and Italy won the match.

From that day Charlie was no longer a great football player. He became worse from match to match. His friends knew what the matter was. They sent him lucky charms, they put horseshoes on the road when Charlie drove to the club. Nothing helped.

One day the club manager got an idea. He put an advertisement in the club paper.

> **Broken Mirrors**
> *Mrs Bunby, just back from the Continent,*
> *will break any unlucky charms.*
> *Apply 36, Christchurch Road, Bromley, Kent.*

Mrs Bunby was an invalid old lady and the manager's aunt. He had told her about his superstitious football player. She was ready to help. Would Charlie read the advertisement? Everybody hoped he would.

As soon as Charlie had read the club paper, he drove to Bromley. Ingrid Müller, Mrs Bunby's German companion, opened the door. She led Charlie into a dark sitting-room where Mrs Bunby was waiting in a wheel-chair. Two black cats were sitting on the table.

"What can I do for you?" asked Mrs Bunby.

"I broke a mirror and since then I've had bad luck," said Charlie.

"You'll have bad luck for seven years if we don't do anything about it." said Mrs Bunby. "But we shall do something about it."

Like a conjuror Mrs Bunby produced a small mirror from her pocket.

"I'll give you this mirror," she said. "It's a lucky charm. Look in it every day and say,

Mirror, mirror on the wall,
I'm the best to kick a ball.

This you'll say three times in the morning, and four times before you go to bed. Seven times in all. Do this and go in peace, my friend. Next Sunday you'll be the best player on the field. Don't tell anyone about the mirror or it won't help you any more."

The following Saturday afternoon the spectators saw a new Charlie Webber. He shot three goals and won the match for his club. And Charlie kept his form. He was sure that Mrs Bunby's mirror brought him good luck.

13. A Race against Time L 24

It was five o'clock in the afternoon of a rainy October day. The car was speeding along a narrow country road when suddenly Bill Walker had to stop. A man was waving his arms and screaming for help.

"What's the matter?" asked Bill Walker.

"Take me to the nearest hospital," cried the stranger. "I've been poisoned. If I don't find a doctor quickly, I'll be dead before night comes."

"Where's the nearest hospital?" asked Bill.

"Brighton," replied the stranger. His face was as white as a sheet.

"Get in," said Bill. "I'll do my best, but Brighton is 30 miles from here."

"I know," groaned the stranger as he sat down in the back of the car. "Please hurry, sir! I've only got an hour to live."

Bill drove at top speed. In the driving-mirror he could see the man's green face.

"How did it happen?" asked Bill. "Was it an accident?"

"It was no accident," groaned the stranger. "My wife did it."

"Did you call the police?"

"No, I didn't. I had no time for that. First I must be taken to a hospital. The police will be called later. Oh, oh, oh! I've an awful pain in my stomach."

It was getting dark. The rain had stopped. Bill switched on the headlights. The stranger in the back was quiet. Another seven miles to Brighton. Would they get to the hospital in time? In the distance Bill could see the lights of Brighton. His passenger was now smoking a cigarette.

"You seem to be better," said Bill.

"I'm much better," replied the stranger.

They were now turning round the corner into the road where Brighton Hospital was.

"Thanks a lot, old man," said the stranger. "It was very kind of you. I'll never forget you and your car."

"Shall I come with you?" asked Bill.

"No, thank you," replied the man. His voice was quiet and normal. "I'll manage it now. I'll walk those few steps alone. Thanks again."

With these words he went up the steps to the hospital entrance and disappeared inside.

Bill waited a little. Something seemed strange about the man. Then he did not trust his eyes. The man was coming out of the hospital hand in hand with a pretty young woman. They were both laughing. That was too much for Bill. He got out of the car, slammed the door and walked up to the couple.

"What's the big idea?" he asked.

"Oh," said the man. "It was a good idea. You see, I had to fetch my wife from Brighton Hospital at six o'clock. She works there. Just when I wanted to start from home, my car broke down. So I stopped the first car on the road and told you that tall story. Will you join us for a drink?"

"I hope you'll join us," said the young woman. "And perhaps, if you go back the same way, you could take us with you again?"

Bill accepted the invitation. "Revenge is sweet," he thought. But the drinks were strong, and Bill had one whisky too many and couldn't drive home. So they all had to stay the night in Brighton.

14. A New Life for Mrs Scott L 25

Gerald Scott's wife was seriously ill. Mr Scott seemed to be very worried about her health. Every day the doctor visited her, but she didn't get better. One day Doctor Brown told the husband that Mrs Scott's trouble was not physical but mental.

"You ought to know best what the trouble is," said the doctor to the husband. "The neighbours say that your marriage is not very happy. They say that you spend your time at the race-course and with other women. Wives sometimes suffer in silence. Your wife is one of those women. Change your way of life, and your wife will soon get better."

"Doctor," answered Mr Scott. "I'm not going to listen to that nonsense. I asked you to help my wife and nothing more."

Two hours later Doctor Brown was again called to the house of the Scotts. Mrs Scott opened the door. She was as white as a sheet. "Come in, Doctor. Quick! My husband is ill. I don't know what has happened."

They went upstairs to the bedroom. Mr Scott was on his bed. His face was grey and he was groaning with pain. He was suffering terribly.

"Quick, Doctor. Help me. I've been poisoned."

"What kind of poison," asked the doctor. "I must know that before I can help you."

"Weed-killer," groaned Mr Scott. "She did it. She wanted to murder me." He pointed to his wife.

Doctor Brown phoned the hospital. Then he called the police. When the police arrived, Mr Scott was already dead. Police Inspector Walker at once began to question Mrs Scott.

Police Inspector: Mrs Scott, you heard your husband's last words. He told the doctor that you had poisoned him.

Mrs Scott: I never did anything of the kind.

Police Inspector: You murdered your husband, because life with him was simply terrible, isn't that so?

Mrs Scott: No, it isn't. I wouldn't murder anyone. I couldn't kill a fly.

Police Inspector: But you could kill your husband.

Mrs Scott: I did not! When Doctor Brown had gone this morning, my husband came to my bedroom with a bottle of whisky and two glasses. He was quite cheerful. He told me that the doctor had said that my trouble was not physical but mental, and that we should start a new life. He filled the two glasses with whisky and handed me one. I asked him to fetch me a cigarette. The cigarettes were downstairs in the living-room. So he put down his glass on the small table at the side of my bed. When he came back I had exchanged our glasses.

Police Inspector: Why did you do that?

Mrs Scott: My glass had more whisky in it. As I don't like whisky very much I just exchanged the glasses while he was downstairs.

Police Inspector: Do you think that he wanted to murder you?

Mrs Scott: I don't know.

Police Inspector:	Was your husband rich?
Mrs Scott:	He hadn't a penny. He got all his money from me.
Police Inspector:	Was there a will in his favour? Did your husband know about it?
Mrs Scott:	Yes, there was a will in his favour and my husband knew about it.
Police Inspector:	Did you tell him that he was poisoned by weed-killer?
Mrs Scott:	How could I know that? He had to tell the doctor that it was weed-killer, because he wanted help. The doctor could not help him if he didn't know what poison it was.

The police inspector now had enough details. His theory was that Mr Scott wanted to murder his wife. The case was closed for the police.

15. Two Strangers Meet L 26

John Turner was a clerk in the City of London. He wasn't rich, but as he didn't spend much he could manage quite well. He lived in a boarding-house near Paddington Station where he had a small room under the roof.

One Saturday evening John Turner put on his best suit, examined the contents of his wallet and decided to go and enjoy himself in the West End.

He phoned for a taxi and told the driver the name of a cinema. In the hall a lot of people were waiting at the box-office. But Turner didn't have to wait. He had bought two expensive tickets the day before. Suddenly a notice went up at the box-office window: 'House Full'.

Turner, with the air of the expert, looked round. He was not going to spend the evening alone. His eyes fell on a bèautiful young lady in an elegant fur coat. Turner addressed her, "Excuse me, you look worried. May I ask you what the trouble is?"

The young lady looked at him. Turner looked harmless enough.

"Well," she said. "I wanted to see that film *Love from a Stranger,* but now I can't. It's house full."

"If I may help you," said Turner. "I've got two tickets for *Love from a Stranger*. I was waiting for my friend. I don't know what has happened to him. He hasn't come. May I make you a present of his ticket?"

"How lovely!" cried the girl. "That's very, very kind of you. What do you want for the ticket?"

"The pleasure of your company," said Turner. "May I introduce myself. My name is John Turner, Doctor Turner."

"I am Betty Gordon. Lord Gordon's youngest daughter. Shall we go in, Doctor Turner?"

Turner was most impressed, for he had never before landed a fish of that kind.

When they came out of the cinema two hours later, Turner turned to his companion. "What about dinner?"

"Oh, I wouldn't say 'no' to a little meal. Let's go to Prunier's. They have wonderful food."

Turner's heart fell into his boots when he looked at the menu. Everything was so terribly expensive, and he only had ten pounds in his wallet.

"I'll order some oysters for myself," said the young lady. "It's the right month for them. And what do you think of a bottle of champagne, Doctor Turner?"

The oysters and the champagne came. They were followed by some excellent veal cutlets, chipped potatoes, and fresh vegetables. Then they had a basket of fruit, sweets and black coffee.

The bill amounted to 15 pounds. Turner became most embarrassed. He knew that he only had ten pounds in his wallet. For a minute or two he wanted to run away, but then he thought better of it. He told the girl that he hadn't enough money on him to pay the bill.

"Is that worrying you?" said the girl. "Let me pay for myself."

She put ten pounds on the table. "Order another bottle of champagne, Doctor Turner. We're going to enjoy ourselves tonight."

Before they parted in Piccadilly Circus Underground Station, the young lady asked Turner for his address. Turner couldn't bring himself to tell her the truth. He gave a wrong address.

On the way home he felt that he had missed the chance of his life.

As soon as she got home, Betty went straight to her neighbour's flat. "I've brought back your fur coat," she said. "Thank you very much. I met a most attractive young doctor and we enjoyed ourselves very much. But I made a fool of myself. I pretended to be Lord Gordon's daughter and later I couldn't bring myself to tell him the truth. I'll never see him again. I've missed the chance of my life."

16. Journey's End

L 27

The policeman came up the dark street slowly. The time was about 10 o'clock and the night was cold.

The policeman, whose job it was to go round the district at this time of night, tried the door of a shop here and there to see if it was shut. As he was moving on, he suddenly saw a man who was standing in the doorway of a shop. The policeman walked up to him.

"It's all right, officer," the man said. "I'm just waiting for a friend. It's an appointment which I made twenty years ago. Let me explain to you. Twenty years ago there was a pub here."

"Yes, the pub was there over the road until five years ago," said the policeman. "Then they put that office building in its place."

The man in the doorway took a match out of a box to light a cigarette. In the light of the match the policeman saw the man's face. It was the face of a man about forty, with blue eyes and full lips.

"Twenty years ago," said the man, "I had a few drinks with Bill Scott, my best friend, in that pub. I was eighteen and Bill was twenty. The next day I was sailing to the USA. I told Bill to go with me, but you couldn't get Bill out of London. That night we decided to meet here again twenty years later on December 20th, at 10 o'clock."

"Have you heard from your friend since then?" asked the policeman.

"Yes, for the first two years," answered the stranger. "But then I heard no more from him."

"Do you think your friend will come?" asked the policeman.

"The man I'm waiting for is the best friend in the world. I came 3,000 miles to see him. If he's alive, he'll come tonight."

"Well," said the policeman. "I hope your friend will come. Are you going to wait long?"

"I give him twenty minutes," said the man in the doorway.

"Well, good night, sir," said the policeman as he left the stranger. And in the doorway the man who had come 3,000 miles to meet his friend, smoked his cigarette and waited.

He waited for about ten minutes, and then a tall man in a long coat hurried over from the opposite side of the street. He went straight to the man.

"Is that you, George?" he asked.

"Is that you, Bill Scott?" answered the man in the door.

"Sure enough, it's George!" shouted the man in the long coat and took the other's hand. "Twenty years is a long time, but I was sure I'd find you here. The old pub's gone, George. So we must look for another. Never mind! Let's go this way. How did you like it in the States, George?"

"I had good luck right from the minute I landed in New York."

When the two men came into the light of a shop window, they both looked at one another.

The man from America stopped suddenly.

"You aren't Bill Scott," he said. "Twenty years is a long time, but not long enough to change blue eyes into black eyes."

"Twenty years can change a good man into a bad character," said the tall man. "You're wanted by the police. Are you coming quietly? Before we go to the police station, here's a piece of paper which I was asked to hand to you. You may read it here at the window." The man from America read the few words which were written on it: 'George, I was at the appointed place in time. When you lighted your cigarette I saw it was the face of a man whom the police wanted to question. I couldn't do it myself, so I went to the station and asked a plain clothes man to do the job.

Bill.'

Adapted from *After Twenty Years* by O. Henry

17. Queen Victoria L 28

Victoria became queen in 1837, when she was eighteen. Three years later she married a German prince, Albert of Saxe-Coburg-Gotha, who was the same age.

Real democracy did not exist in Britain at the time of her coronation. Life was very hard for the poor whose children had to work in factories and did not go to school.

When the Queen died in 1901 many of these things had changed for the better, but there was still a lot to do in the social field.

Victoria ruled the greatest Empire the world had ever seen. She became Empress of India in 1876. It was the most magnificent ceremony that had taken place in Britain for a long time. The British Empire had reached the height of its power. For many Englishmen the future seemed wonderful. "All the days were good and each day better than the other," young Churchill wrote in his book *My Early Life*.

The constitutional duties the Queen had to fulfil and the mass of documents she had to deal with made her a very busy woman. Her life was a time-table that she observed to the minute.

Though she was happily married and loved her husband, there were often quarrels between her and Prince Albert. The Queen was a very proud woman and she sometimes tried to play the sovereign even in her private life.

One evening, at dinner, Victoria told Albert that he should not go to the Houses of Parliament the next day. Albert did not like the way she ordered him about. He got up from his meal, went to his private room and turned the key of the door behind him. The Queen, however, found such behaviour impossible and soon knocked at Albert's door.

"Open the door at once," she ordered, "The Queen wants to speak to you."

There was no answer. Victoria knocked a second time.

"Who's there?" Albert asked.—"The Queen of England."

Again there was no answer. Victoria knocked and knocked. The questions and the answers were repeated several times. But the door was not opened. Victoria stood in front of it, her face as red as a beetroot. What could she do? Finally she knocked again, but this time it was a different knock, not hard but worried and shy.

"Who's there?" asked the Prince.

"Your wife, Albert."

And the door was at once opened to Victoria.

18. A Worker's Family at the Time of Queen Victoria

L 29

Manchester, 1846. A dark room in a poor, narrow street was the home of the Robinsons, a family of eight. They had been ten, but two of the eight children had died. No doctor had attended them.

Six days a week John Robinson and his wife Nancy left the house at four o'clock in the morning to walk two miles to the factory where they worked. John was a fitter, Nancy a packer. It was not before seven in the evening that they came back from their day's work, tired and hungry.

As the parents did not earn enough money, the children had to work too.

Fifteen-year-old Jack worked in a brickfield. Fourteen hours a day he carried heavy bricks and he was proud when he brought his wages home.

Tom, thirteen years of age, was a chimney-sweep. When he climbed inside the big chimneys, he often lost his way. Not that it worried him, for he was as much at home in a dark chimney as a mouse is underground.

Mary was employed in the same factory as her parents. As she was only ten, she worked eight hours a day. She was rather a small girl and her job was to creep under the machines and clean them.

Children under the age of nine were not allowed to work in factories. So the three younger Robinsons stayed at home and made matchboxes. The wages were $2\frac{1}{2}$ d. for 144 boxes.

No child had ever been to school. They could not read or write. They had not time to play in the street and had never been outside Manchester.

If illness or unemployment came, the workhouse was waiting for the Robinsons. Husband and wife, brothers and sisters, children and parents had to part. They had to live in different departments of this prison for the poor. They feared it all their lives. It was worse than death for them.

19. Noise in the Night L 30

Every Christmas the Appletons stayed at Mrs Green's. They were not the only guests in that large country house, for Mrs Green liked to have company from Christmas Eve to New Year's Day. There were evenings with card-playing, party games and laughter. The rooms were decorated with balloons, holly and mistletoe. There was plenty of drink and food.

Only Marilyn, the Appletons' sixteen-year-old daughter, was bored. Tom and Bill, two cousins of hers, with whom she had hoped to enjoy herself under the mistletoe, had not come that year. Instead she had to be with people whose company she did not find very entertaining. There was one guest, however, who was really impossible—Mrs Pebblestone. She was a woman of sixty, very big, very loud and very important. She was a friend of Mrs Green's. Marilyn's room was next to hers. As the walls were thin, the girl could hear all the noises next door: the snoring which began as soon as the lady was in bed, the alarm clock at 5.30 (the lady rose early), the water which was running into the bath, the maid who brought the early morning tea, the radio that gave the first news.

After three sleepless nights Marilyn took a sleeping-tablet. It did not help her very much, for the snoring next door was so loud. Marilyn knocked against the wall. The snoring stopped for a minute, then started again louder than ever. At last Marilyn got up to go downstairs and sleep in the sitting-room. The time was one o'clock. As she passed her neighbour's room, Marilyn saw a notice which hung on the door: "Early morning tea at five, please!" Marilyn took the notice from the door and went back to her room. There she took another piece of paper on which she wrote, "The end has come! Send my body to Wimbledon Crematorium. Sorry for the trouble."

Very quietly Marilyn hung up the new message over her neighbour's door. Then she took a paper bag, filled it with air, and broke it against the staircase wall. The noise was terrible. All the dogs in the house began to howl. Soon everybody was up. When they came to Hilda Pebblestone's door they discovered the message.

"She's taken her life," said Mr Appleton. "I heard the noise of a gun. We must break into the room."

The noise outside her room awoke Hilda Pebblestone. She opened the door.

"What's going on here?" she asked.

They showed her the notice.

"I don't like jokes of that kind," she said and slammed the door of her room in their faces.

Next morning she told Mrs Green that she would never spend another Christmas in her house. She was sure that Mr Green had wanted to make a fool of her because he did not like her. She left after breakfast.

The night after Mrs Pebblestone's departure Marilyn slept very well.

Adapted from *Reginald's Christmas Revel* by Saki

20. English Habits

L 31

When I went to see my friend Appleby I found him in the kitchen. He was peeling potatoes. "Sit down, old boy," he said. "Supper will be ready in half an hour."

I sat down and questioned him about his duties as a housewife. Like many other English husbands, Appleby not only brings his wife a cup of tea in the morning, but also helps her in the house every day, sometimes cooks supper in the evening, and carries the bags when she goes shopping on Saturdays.

"What would happen if you didn't do all this?" I asked.

"I don't know," answered Appleby. "If I hadn't helped my wife all these years, she wouldn't look as young as she does."

In the living-room I found Mrs Appleby. She was sitting on the floor and was surrounded by fifty coloured Christmas cards.

"Come in!" she said. "I'm addressing my Christmas cards and you can help with the stamps."

I sat down on the very hard floor and put the stamps on the envelopes.

The English send Christmas cards to everyone they know. They send one to their neighbour next door, one to the people they met three years ago on holiday, one to Tom, Dick or Harry.

There are two reasons why the English send so many cards with "Merry Christmas and a Happy New Year". First, it is an English custom. Second, if you send a lot of Christmas cards, you'll also get a lot. People put them on the mantelpiece and proudly show them to their friends when they call.

I did not enjoy Appleby's efforts as a cook. After supper we went for a drink at the *Red Lion*. Some friends of Appleby's joined us. They all ordered rounds. When it was my turn, I had to pay for six drinks. I drank more than I really wanted. If it hadn't been for that habit of rounds, I would only have drunk two glasses of beer instead of six. After that we all got into our cars and drove to another pub. At eleven we had to leave the pub because it was closing time. I took a taxi to the big West End hotel, where I was staying.

When I came to the breakfast room in the morning there was a long queue at the door. The English love to queue up. I looked into the breakfast room and saw that there were quite a number of tables free. I wanted to go in, but the waiter stopped me.

"What's wrong with all those tables?" I asked.

"Nothing, sir, if I may say so. But those are tables for two. You need a table for one, sir. If you don't mind, sir, you'll have to wait a little."

I waited for twenty minutes and then was led to a small table for one. While I was sitting at my breakfast table I took my newspaper and tried to read it, but I had to be careful. The pages were so big and the tables so near to each other that I almost covered up my neighbour's eggs and bacon. So I gave it up and read my paper after breakfast in the large hotel hall where there were plenty of comfortable seats.

21. A Visit to Stratford-on-Avon L 32

August 29, 1971

Dear Barbara,

Leaving London from Paddington Station in the 10.30 train to Birmingham, I had lunch in the dining-car and had just finished my meal when I arrived at Leamington Spa where I had to change for Stratford-on-Avon.

An hour later I was walking through this pleasant little market town with its half-timbered houses, many dating from the time of Queen Elizabeth I. I had time to see the house where Shakespeare was born in 1564, to visit the Grammar School where as a schoolboy he learned "little Latin and less Greek"* and the garden of New Place where the poet spent the last years of his life.

In front of the Royal Theatre a lot of people were queueing, hoping to get seats for the afternoon performance. Having booked well in advance, I had the ticket in my wallet. The Royal Theatre is a red brick building, lying by the side of the famous River Avon. The sun shining on the blue waters of the river, the green trees and meadows, made a pretty picture. All that I would have seen with greater pleasure if you had been with me.

Having booked for the gallery, I climbed the steps to my seat under the roof. Would I be able to hear well? I didn't have to worry about that. As soon as the curtain rose, I could hear every word coming from the stage. Of course, I wasn't able to understand everything. However, having read the play in German, I managed to follow.

It was five o'clock when I came out of the theatre. I still had more than an hour before my train left for London. So I walked along the river to Holy Trinity Church which lies a short distance from the town. The sun was in the west, and through the coloured church windows its light fell on the tombstone where Shakespeare rests beside his wife.

On his grave I read the words written by himself. He asks that his dust should be left in peace, ending with the lines:

"Blessed be the man that spares these stones,
And cursed be he that moves my bones."

Leaving Stratford just before seven, I was back in London shortly after ten o'clock, a little tired but pleased to have seen the birthplace of the world's greatest dramatist who "was not of an age, but for all time."*

Yours,
Hans

* Ben Jonson (1572–1637), poet.

22. A Performance at the Stratford Royal Theatre L 33

September 5, 1971

Dear Barbara,

How right you are! What a fool I was to forget to tell you about the play I saw at the Royal Theatre. It was *As You Like It.* The central figure of this comedy is Rosalind, one of the most charming of Shakespeare's female characters. The play is a love story from beginning to end told in a very entertaining way. It was quite the best performance I've ever seen.

The play is full of funny questions and funny answers. But there are also lines of a more serious character. What impressed me most was the speech beginning with "All the world's a stage, and all the men and women merely players." Shakespeare goes on to say that in his life one man plays many parts. Seven in all:

First the baby crying in the nurse's arms. Then the schoolboy, with his satchel and well-washed face, going slowly and unwillingly to school. The next part is that of the lover, singing love-songs to his darling girl. Then the soldier, looking everywhere for fame. After that the judge, full of good food and good advice. Then the old man, his trousers too big for his thin legs, has lost his manly voice. The last scene of all, that ends this strange story, is second childhood. No teeth, no eyes, no taste—nothing.

"Such is the way of life," I thought. "We all do play one of those seven parts sooner or later." On the stage Rosalind had found her lover, the fool was having his jokes, and the spectators were enjoying themselves.

When I came out of the theatre I felt that my day excursion to Stratford-on-Avon was the finest thing I would enjoy in England. "A thing of beauty is a joy for ever."*

Much love,

Yours,

Hans

* John Keats (1795–1821), poet.

23. Good-bye, Charlie! L 34

It was Cup Final Day. The sun was shining on the crowd of 100,000 spectators. The military band had just finished playing. The Queen was in her seat, and on the green lawn of Wembley her husband, Prince Philip, was shaking hands with the two teams, Luton Town and Nottingham Forest.

Then the match began. It was the fight of two great football clubs. Luton succeeded first in shooting a goal, but then Charlie Webber of Nottingham Forest broke through the lines of Luton and finished his race by kicking the ball into Luton's net. 1—1. Eighty minutes of great football had already passed when Charlie Webber stood again in front of Luton's goal. Charlie jumped and the ball was in the net again. Ten minutes later Charlie and his team received the Cup from the hands of the Queen.

The next day the train with the men of Nottingham Forest on board entered Nottingham Station. The weather was wet and cold, and yet, by coach, by car and on foot the people of Nottingham had come to the station to welcome their team. Men and boys, young girls and their mothers were standing on the station platforms and in the station square like sardines in a tin. Church bells rang, shouts of excitement filled the air. When the Forest Men appeared in their red football shirts, they were in danger of being trampled to death. In no time their shirts were pulled off their bodies. Fortunately it had stopped raining, but it took them half an hour to reach the waiting coaches.

The next day the phone rang at Charlie Webber's home.

It was the club manager.

"We've received an offer for you. It's the biggest sum ever offered for a player," said the manager. "And I don't mind telling you that we've accepted, Charlie, my boy."

"Who wants to buy me?" Charlie asked.

"Manchester City. They'll pay £120,000."

"But I object to leaving," said Charlie.

"Don't be a fool, Charlie," replied the manager. "This is the opportunity of becoming rich over night, Charlie, my boy. Both for you and for the club."

"You're selling me for £120,000. That's like selling and buying a slave."

"No, Charlie, it isn't. It's big business. People will enjoy watching you play football in Manchester just as they did in Nottingham. And you'll get a beautiful house, a new car and double the money we pay you here. What do you say to this?"

"Well, that's different, boss. I don't mind accepting the offer in such case."

"That's it, Charlie. I expect you to be at my office tomorrow at ten. Good-bye, Charlie."

24. Teaching by Telephone

L 35

Foreign Languages Ltd
White House Road
Wolverhampton

Tel. Wolverhampton 27 65

Your Ref.

Our Ref. JMCT/MW
23 June 1971

Mrs M. Wheatley
Tree Tops
Codsall/Wolverhampton

Dear Mrs Wheatley,

We corresponded last year about your becoming a teacher by telephone for *Foreign Languages*.

We have now quite a number of students learning by this method and it is proving very successful.

Three members of the staff of a Wolverhampton tyre factory wish to start learning German by telephone and we wonder whether you would like to take on the job of teaching them.

We have pleasure in enclosing our book *Learning German by Telephone* and suggest your beginning with Lesson 1 on June 30 when the students will ring you up for their first lesson. No lesson should last longer than half an hour. Each student has booked for a course of 20 lessons which have been paid for in advance. Your fees will be £1.90 for each lesson.

We should be grateful if you could let us know as soon as possible whether you would undertake this work.

Yours sincerely,
J. M. C. Taylor
Director

Tree Tops
Codsall/Wolverhampton
Tel. Wolverhampton 29 76

J. M. C. Taylor, Esq.
Foreign Languages Ltd
Wolverhampton

June 26, 1971

Dear Mr Taylor,

Your Ref. JMCT/MW

Thank you for your letter of the 23rd inst. I am prepared to accept your offer to teach three students German by telephone. Please let me know the exact time of their calling me on June 30.

Yours sincerely,
(Mrs) M. Wheatley

25. A Man Called Smith

L 36/37

"Your future father-in-law is going to call on you this afternoon without telling you who he is. I just wanted to prepare you for the big event," said a woman's voice on the phone.

"Who's speaking?" replied Freddie Wiggs.

There was no answer and Freddie put down the receiver. Well, if his future father-in-law was paying a visit, Freddie would be prepared. He told his secretary to go and fetch a bottle of whisky, some expensive cigars, and something tasty to eat. Then he phoned his friend Tom.

"Look here, Tom. Should I phone you this afternoon, don't be surprised that you'll be my business partner in New York I'll be talking to. It's important. Thank you."

About four o'clock his secretary came into his office.

"A gentleman wants to speak to you, sir," she announced. "His name is Smith."

His girl-friend's family name was Smith, too. Now Freddie knew. His future father-in-law was calling on him to find out what kind of man his daughter wanted to marry. As the gentleman of about fifty came in, Freddie welcomed him like an old friend, asked him to sit down, offered him some whisky and pushed some cigars under his nose.

"I hope you won't mind waiting some minutes, sir," Freddie told his visitor. "I've got an important call to New York. These Americans have put up their prices for tinned sausages. I must speak to them."

Freddie phoned the number of his friend in London.

"Now that you can dial the New York number, you get through directly," he told the gentleman who was quietly smoking his cigar. "Hello, is that Johnson and Co, New York? May I speak to the managing director, please? This is Wiggs, London, speaking. Hello, is that you, Bob? Look here, old man. Your sausage prices are up again. Have you forgotten that I bought £50,000 worth of sausages from you last year? Listen, Bob. If you can't sell at last year's prices, somebody else will. I mean it, Bob. I'll give you another day to think it over. I've got an order on my desk for $70,000. Anyone will be glad to get it, Bob. Take it or leave it. Yes, call me any time tomorrow between four and five. I'll be at the office. Kind regards to the wife. Bye, Bob."

Freddie hung up.

"Your business seems to be very good, sir," said the gentleman.

"It is," said Freddie. "I've got one of the largest sausage firms in the country. Last year I spent more than £10,000 on advertising. This year I'll spend £20,000. I've been in the business for more than five years and since then I've never looked back."

"You said you gave an order of £50,000 to Johnson and Co, New York last year. Is that right?"

"That's right, sir. Have another whisky."

"Thanks, I will."

"It's the best twelve-year-old Scotch I've ever had. It goes on the expenses."

"Would it be asking too much if I asked you how big your net income was last year?"

"Not at all, sir. Last year my net income was £6,000. This year it'll be a little more. There's a lot of money in sausages, believe me, sir."

"I'm quite prepared to believe it, Mr Wiggs," said the gentleman. "Especially when meat and bread are well mixed together. There's just one question I'd like to ask you. How is it that with all that business you only declared an income of £1,000 to the tax office?"

Freddie was most surprised.

"How do you know?" he asked.

"Well," said the gentleman rising from his seat. "You see, I'm a tax inspector. I've come to your office to make some inquiries about last year's income-tax return. But now, I've got all the information I need. By the way, your whisky is really first class and your cigars are very good indeed. Good afternoon, sir."

26. London

L 38

The huge city gets bigger and bigger. Every year thousands and thousands of people from Ireland, Wales and Scotland will take the one-way train to the capital.

Many of them think that the streets of London are covered with gold, that they only have to pick it up to become wealthy and rich. True, there are high wages in London, people of the same professions earn more money there than anywhere else in Britain, but the cost of living is high, too. And life is not much more attractive in the South-east of England than anywhere else.

George Londoner gets up at six o'clock five times a week. He is to be at his office in the City at nine. He rushes to the bathroom, dresses quickly, has breakfast, gets his car out of the garage and drives some miles to Caterham Station, Surrey, where he leaves it and takes the train to the City.

In the South-east of England 700,000 other commuters will travel daily to Central London in the morning and back to their suburbs in the evening. They will lunch in crowded restaurants, small pubs, in canteens, or may eat their sandwiches in their offices or in parks. Every week-day they will spend three to four hours in crowded buses, undergrounds, trains and cars.

Do they like this kind of life? Of course they don't. An official report says that 42 per cent of men working in London would leave the South-east if they could find good jobs in the West. But can they? Before the Second World War the City of London was a place filled by small offices, huge warehouses, wonderful old churches, little corners and narrow streets. Then came the blitz and quite a number of these went up in the air. So much of what was left has been swept away by large new office buildings round St. Paul's Cathedral that the face of the City has completely changed.

These huge new buildings draw the commuters from the suburbs to the City which has a day population of 440,000 and a night population of only 5,000. So the dream of thousands of Londoners, the dream of going West and leaving the capital, will never come true, for the new big office buildings in Central London will never be empty and won't let them go.

27. A Letter from America

L 39

June 21, 1971

Dear Mother,

I always knew that many things in the USA were better and bigger than anywhere else. I knew that the USA has as many motorcars as Britain has inhabitants. The highest building in the world is the Empire State Building in New York. The largest hotel is the Hilton in Chicago with 3,000 rooms. The Pentagon in Washington, the USA Department of Defence, employs about 30,000 people and has 44,000 telephones, and the world's biggest railway station is the Grand Central Terminal in New York, etc., etc.

But the other day something surprised me. The dog cult has always been looked upon as the Englishman's special craze. Dogs' cemeteries are taken care of from the south of England to the north of Scotland. The bulldog is a national symbol. Even American friends told me, "You English are crazy about dogs." I proudly agreed.

But then I read in the newspapers that we British were no longer leading the world in the dog craze. Statistics tell me that Americans are twice as crazy. Another of our proud titles gone to America!

Over here there are 28 million dogs, against four million in Britain. Of course America has a bigger human population, but it's not seven times as big. One British family in four has a dog. Over here there is one in every second household and the numbers are still going up. Seven out of every ten American dogs are blue-blooded.

Dogs service firms where dog sitters and dog walkers have become new professions, where dog shoes, dog coats and dog suits are bought, where the pets are given their baths and special food, can be found in every quarter of any town in the States.

Dog food factories are doing wonderful trade. Their TV advertisements are almost non-stop. The amount of space given to dog foods in the supermarkets is larger than anything known in Britain. Dogs are the number one customers of the American tinned food industry.

While in Britain more and more smaller dogs are preferred, the Americans want to have bigger and bigger ones. Favourites are the Great Danes, St. Bernards and the Old English Sheepdogs. Here again everything is bigger than anywhere else.

Well, Mother, it's no use giving your dachshund more food. He hasn't a chance against those American superdogs.

Your loving son,
John

28. Compromise throughout the Centuries L 40/41/42

The English have always had a talent for compromise. It is one of their national characteristics and has been formed by long historic training.

When Parliament came into being in the 13th century there was only one big assembly where the King, the great barons, the knights and citizens sat together. It was natural in the beginning that the knights and citizens were there to be seen but not heard unless the King wanted them to speak. The situation was rather a difficult one for the knights. If they supported the King, the great barons might be angry as their interests were often very different from those of the King. So it was not surprising that eventually the knights and citizens retired to a wing of Westminster Palace to debate freely among themselves. When they had agreed, they chose a Speaker to speak for them before the King and the barons.

This custom of debating first among themselves and then sending a Speaker to the King and the barons led to the two-chamber system, the House of Lords and the House of Commons.

Today the Speaker in the House of Commons is a highly desired and well-paid position. Nevertheless each time a new Speaker has been elected a little comedy takes place. The new Speaker pretends to refuse his post and has to be pushed to the chair by several other members. This dates from the time when to be Speaker was not at all pleasant, as quite a number of those gentlemen were executed.

The House of Commons was composed of the landed gentry and townspeople. The interests of the two groups differed very often, but if the House of Commons wanted to survive in the face of the mighty barons and the King, there could not be quarrels of life and death between town and country. Landed gentry and citizens learned how to compromise. They got accustomed to being together and to settling their different opinions by debating.

But also the House of Lords had its connections with the House of Commons. Only the eldest son of a lord inherited the title, the property and the seat in the House of Lords from his father. The younger sons were just ordinary citizens who often sat in the House of Commons. It is clear that the many family connections between the House of Lords and the House of Commons made compromise easier. Brothers will rarely fight each other in the same way as strangers do. The French Revolution with all its cruelty would never have been possible with the English. Too many links connected and still connect one social class with the other ones. As the power of the House of Lords decreased so much that today it may be the end of a political career for a man to inherit the title from his father, a compromise has been found again. The son of a lord need not accept the title any more. On the other hand elderly statesmen are often honoured by becoming members of the House of Lords. Herbert Morrison, a former milkman and, later, chairman of the Labour Party, in his old age became Lord Morrison of Lambeth. Herbert Morrison was only one example of many and the House of Lords has a large number of members belonging to the Labour Party.

In the course of centuries the power of the Crown also decreased. The monarchy, however, was not abolished as in many other European countries, but a compromise was found to make parliamentary democracy and constitutional monarchy work together. The absolute monarch of former times has become a representative of the people today.

Compromise is also to be found in the way Britain solved her Empire problem. Instead of fighting for her colonies as the French did in Vietnam and Algeria, the British did not oblige any country to remain a member of the Commonwealth. Only once did Britain not observe the rules of compromise in her history with the colonies and she suffered a set-back, even a very serious one: the loss of her American colonies. This taught the English a lesson. When in the 19th century Canada showed signs of unrest, Britain was ready to compromise and granted home rule to this vast colony. The change from Empire to Commonwealth is the story of compromise. This attitude saved Britain a lot of trouble.

Looking back on this historical development, in which the gift of compromise has played such an important part, we may well ask whether it was Parliament that made England or England that made Parliament.

Wörterverzeichnis

1. Christmas Presents

7	Christmas ['krisməs]	Weihnachten
	present ['preznt]	Geschenk
	to enter ['entə]	betreten, eintreten
	store [stɔ:]	Kaufhaus
	to provide [prə'vaid]	besorgen, liefern
	everything ['evriθing]	alles
	haircut ['hɛəkʌt]	Haarschnitt
	honeymoon ['hʌnimu:n]	Hochzeitsreise, Flitterwochen
	if	wenn, falls
	money ['mʌni]	Geld
	to dream [dri:m]	träumen
	expensive [iks'pensiv]	teuer
	detective [di'tektiv]	Detektiv
	office ['ɔfis]	Büro, Arbeitszimmer
	*near the entrance** ['niə ði 'entrəns]	*nahe beim Eingang*
	to watch [wɔtʃ]	beobachten
	different ['difrənt]	verschieden
	department [di'pɑ:tmənt]	(Verkaufs-) Abteilung
	television [teli'viʒən]	Fernsehen
	she looks sweet [swi:t]	*sie sieht süß aus*
	fair hair ['fɛə 'hɛə]	blondes Haar
	slim figure ['figə]	schlanke Figur
	shirt [ʃə:t]	Hemd
	tie [tai]	Krawatte, Schlips
	sock	Socke
	assistant [ə'sistənt]	Verkäufer, -in
	shock	Schock, Schreck
	to forget [fə'get]	vergessen
	to pay [pei]	bezahlen
	to leave [li:v]	verlassen
	to marry ['mæri]	heiraten
	sad [sæd]	traurig
	another [ə'nʌðə]	ein anderer
	happy ['hæpi]	glücklich
	wedding ['wediŋ]	Hochzeit

2. Grandma Sophia

8	grandma ['grænmɑ:]	Großmutter
	Sophia [sə'fiə]	*ital. Vorname*
	Belgian ['beldʒən]	belgisch, Belgier
	boat [bəut]	Boot, Schiff, Dampfer
	Dover Harbour ['dəuvə 'hɑ:bə]	Hafen von Dover
	passenger ['pæsindʒə]	Passagier
	luggage ['lʌgidʒ]	Gepäck
	Italian [i'tæljən]	italienisch, Italiener
	signora, *ital.* [sin'jɔ:rə]	Frau
	Capone [kə'pəuni]	*ital. Familienname*
	customs hall ['kʌstəmz hɔ:l]	Zollabfertigung
	suitcase ['sju:tkeis]	Koffer
	which suitcase is yours?	*welcher Koffer gehört Ihnen?*
	customs officer ['ɔfisə]	Zollbeamter
	to point to [pɔint]	zeigen auf
	to declare ['di'klɛə]	verzollen
	camera ['kæmərə]	Kamera, Fotoapparat
	nothing at all	*überhaupt nichts*
	watch	Uhr
	ten in all	*insgesamt zehn*
	to produce [prə'dju:s]	zum Vorschein bringen, hervorbringen
	cigarette-case [sigə'retkeis]	Zigarettenetui
	main office ['mein 'ɔfis]	Hauptbüro
	train [trein]	Eisenbahnzug
	customs, *Mehrz.* ['kʌstəmz]	Zoll
	to arrive [ə'raiv]	ankommen
	child, children [tʃaild, 'tʃildrən]	Kind, Kinder
	to welcome ['welkəm]	willkommen heißen
	smile [smail]	Lächeln
	never mind, dear ['nevə 'maind diə]	*mach dir nichts draus, meine Liebe; macht nichts, meine Liebe*

* Idiomatische Wendungen sind *kursiv* gedruckt.

better luck next time [lʌk]	mehr Glück beim nächsten Mal
idea [ai'diə]	Idee
Brighton ['braitn]	*Seebad an der Kanalküste*
pier [piə]	in die See hinausragender Promenadensteg
beauty competition ['bju:ti kɔmpə'tiʃən]	Schönheitswettbewerb
the most attractive [ə'træktiv]	die attraktivste
to walk [wɔ:k]	(spazieren)gehen
grandchildren ['græntʃildrən]	Enkelkinder
in front of [in 'frʌnt‿əv]	vor
judge [dʒʌdʒ]	(Preis-)Richter
What chance has Grandma Sophia got?	*Welche Chance hat Oma Sofia?*
dress [dres]	Kleid
behind [bi'haind]	hinter
parade [pə'reid]	Parade, Vorbeimarsch, Vorführung
to win	gewinnen
to give out	verteilen
prize [praiz]	Preis
picture ['piktʃə]	Bild
newspaper ['nju:speipə]	Zeitung
copy ['kɔpi]	Exemplar, Abschrift
Rome [rəum]	Rom

3. A Sunday Morning Dream

9 dream [dri:m]	Traum
Mary ['mɛəri]	Maria
married couple [mærid 'kʌpl]	verheiratetes Paar, Ehepaar
flat [flæt]	(Etagen-)Wohnung
ideal [ai'diəl]	ideal
husband ['hʌzbənd]	Gatte
in the morning	*morgens*
breakfast at her bedside ['brekfəst]	*Frühstück an ihrem Bett*
to wash up the dishes ['wɔʃ‿'ʌp]	*Geschirr abwaschen*
to be slimming	*eine Schlankheitskur machen*
church clock ['tʃə:tʃklɔk]	Kirchenuhr
to strike [straik]	schlagen
to switch on	andrehen
programme ['prəugræm]	Programm
boring [bɔ:riŋ]	langweilig
to fetch	holen
front door ['frʌnt dɔ:]	Haustür
sitting-room ['sitiŋrum]	Wohnzimmer
interesting ['intrestiŋ]	interessant
actor ['æktə]	Schauspieler
champagne [ʃæm'pein]	Sekt
waiter ['weitə]	Kellner
cake [keik]	Kuchen
flower ['flauə]	Blume
Rolls Royce ['rəulz 'rɔis]	*teuerste englische Automarke*
chair ['tʃɛə]	Stuhl
mirror ['mirə]	Spiegel
beautiful [bju:təful]	schön
too [tu:]	auch
face [feis]	Gesicht
West End ['west 'end]	*Vergnügungs- und Repräsentationsviertel von London*
Italy ['itəli]	Italien
holidays ['hɔlədiz]	Ferien, Urlaub
to spend, spent, spent [e]	verbringen
cheap [tʃi:p]	billig
guest-house ['gesthaus]	Pension, Gasthaus
station ['steiʃən]	Bahnhof
guest [gest]	Gast
people [pi:pl]	Leute
like [laik]	wie
family ['fæmili]	Familie
to dream [dri:m]	träumen
to drive [draiv]	fahren
Wimbledon ['wimbldən]	*Vorort von London*
garden [gɑ:dn]	Garten
at that moment ['məumənt]	in diesem Augenblick
voice [vɔis]	Stimme
free [fri:]	frei

4. The Girl Next Door

the girl next door [gə:l]	*das Mädchen von nebenan* 10
gentleman, *Mehrz.* -men ['dʒentlmən]	Herr

boat train ['bəut‿trein]	Schiffsanschlußzug
address [ə'dres]	Adresse
Warwick Terrace ['wɔrik 'terəs]	*Name einer Straße*
central ['sentrəl]	zentral(gelegen)
landlady ['lændleidi]	Wirtin
widow ['widəu]	Witwe
you'll be very happy there	*Sie werden dort sehr glücklich sein*
to look for	suchen nach
number ['nʌmbə]	Nummer
thin [θin]	dünn
lady ['leidi]	Dame
orange-coloured ['ɔrindʒ'kʌləd]	orangefarben
dark [dɑ:k]	dunkel
roof [ru:f]	Dach
to stay [stei]	bleiben
to decide [di'said]	beschließen, sich entschließen
awful ['ɔ:ful]	schrecklich
neighbour ['neibə]	Nachbar
to pass [pɑ:s]	vorbeiziehen, vergehen
to wait for [weit]	warten auf
heart [hɑ:t]	Herz
expectation [ekspek'teiʃən]	Erwartung
I wondered what she was like ['wʌndə]	*ich fragte mich, wie sie aussehe*
to meet [mi:t]	treffen, begegnen
I heard [hə:d]	ich hörte
noise [nɔiz]	Geräusch, Lärm
outside my room ['aut'said]	vor meinem Zimmer
to rush [rʌʃ]	eilen
eye [ai]	Auge
maid [meid]	Dienstmädchen
ill	krank
to have a cold [kəuld]	*erkältet sein*
to reply [ri'plai]	erwidern
to need [ni:d]	brauchen
another [ə'nʌðə]	noch einen, einen weiteren
boarding-house ['bɔ:diŋhaus]	Pension
to laugh [lɑ:f]	lachen
mouse-trap ['maustræp]	Mausefalle

5. Aunt Lily's Letter

letter ['letə]	Brief	11
aunt [ɑ:nt]	Tante	
relative ['relətiv]	Verwandter	
nephew ['nevju]	Neffe	
to keep, kept, kept [i:, e]	(be)halten	
to keep s.o. company ['kʌmpəni]	*jdm. Gesellschaft leisten*	
July [dʒu'lai]	Juli	
to go shopping ['ʃɔpiŋ]	*einkaufen gehen*	
hot [hɔt]	heiß	
to phone [fəun]	anrufen, telefonieren	
burglar ['bə:glə]	Einbrecher	
to call	rufen, hier: vorbeikommen	
to steal, stole, stolen [sti:l, stəul, 'stəulən]	stehlen	
fur coat ['fə: 'kəut]	Pelzmantel	
sugar ['ʃugə]	Zucker	
marmalade ['mɑ:məleid]	Orangenmarmelade	
cat [kæt]	Katze	
kitten ['kitn]	junges Kätzchen	
armchair ['ɑ:m'tʃɛə]	Sessel	
by the way	*nebenbei bemerkt*	
to drink, drank, drunk [i, æ, ʌ]	trinken	
rum [rʌm]	Rum	
glass [glɑ:s]	Glas	
of course [əv'kɔ:s]	natürlich	
he couldn't ['kudnt]	er konnte nicht	
to watch [wɔtʃ]	beobachten	
to take no notice ['nəutis]	keine Notiz nehmen	
to pull a long face ['pul‿ə‿lɔŋ 'feis]	*ein langes Gesicht machen*	
cook [kuk]	Köchin	
tinned [tind]	in, aus Dosen, Büchsen-	
for supper ['sʌpə]	zum Abendessen	
tomato soup [tə'mɑ:təu su:p]	Tomatensuppe	
potato, *Mehrz.* -oes [pə'teitəu]	Kartoffel	
boarder ['bɔ:də]	Pensionsgast	
difficult ['difikəlt]	schwierig	
fortunately ['fɔ:tʃnətli]	glücklicherweise	
to miss	vermissen	
love from [lʌv]	liebe Grüße von	

6. Derby Day in Epsom

12 Derby [ˈdʌ:bi]	*Eigenname*
Epsom [ˈepsəm]	*Stadt südl. von London*
this is George Taylor speaking [ˈdʒɔ:dʒ ˈteilə]	*hier spricht George Taylor*
to report [riˈpɔ:t]	berichten, Bericht erstatten
race [reis]	Rennen
race-course [ˈreiskɔ:s]	Rennplatz
three-year-old horses [hɔ:siz]	dreijährige Pferde
queen [kwi:n]	Königin
royal [rɔiəl]	königlich
colour television [ˈkʌlə teliˈviʒən]	Farbfernsehen
to wear, wore, worn [wɛə, wɔ:, wɔ:n]	tragen (von Kleidern)
pink	rosa
slim	schlank
a few [ə ˈfju:]	einige
Britain [ˈbritn]	Britannien
chance [tʃɑ:ns]	Chance, Aussicht
to win, won, won [win, wʌn]	gewinnen
it's your turn [tə:n]	*Sie sind an der Reihe*
good luck to you all	*Euch allen viel Glück*
to back the right horse	*auf das richtige Pferd setzen*
kind [kaind]	freundlich
to play [plei]	spielen
good-bye [ˈgudˈbai]	auf Wiedersehen, leb wohl
lovely [ˈlʌvli]	hübsch
they are off	*ab sind sie, sie sind gestartet*
corner [ˈkɔ:nə]	Ecke
Royal Fly [ˈrɔiəl ˈflai]	*Name eines Pferdes*
to lead, led, led [i:, e]	führen, anführen
field [fi:ld]	Feld
French	französisch, Franzose
close behind [kləus biˈhaind]	dicht dahinter
still five hundred yards to go	*noch fünfhundert Yards bis zum Ziel*
yard [jɑ:d]	Yard (ca. 90 cm)
in front [ʌ]	vorne
Dublin [ˈdʌblin]	*hier: Name eines Pferdes*
Irish [ˈaiəriʃ]	irisch
winning-post [ˈwiniŋpəust]	Ziel
to shoot, shot, shot [u:, ɔ]	schießen
like an arrow [ærəu]	wie ein Pfeil
to overtake, -took, -taken [əuvəˈteik, u, ei]	überholen
royal colours [ˈrɔiəl ˈkʌləz]	königliche Farben
winner	Sieger

7. Tom and Shirley

Shirley [ˈʃə:li]	*weibl. Vorname* 13
Bromley [ˈbrɔmli]	*Vorstadt östl. von London*
Home, sweet home	*trautes Heim, Glück allein*
motto [ˈmɔtəu]	Wahlspruch
sweet [swi:t]	Süßigkeit
to hand [hænd]	übergeben, aushändigen
sweets for the sweet	*Süßigkeiten für die Süße*
during [ˈdju:riŋ]	während
something [ˈsʌmθiŋ]	etwas
to water [ˈwɔ:tə]	begießen
some [sʌm]	einige
curtain [ˈkə:tn]	Vorhang
to hang up [hæŋ ˈʌp]	aufhängen
carpet [ˈkɑ:pit]	Teppich
to nail down [neil ˈdaun]	annageln
just [dʒʌst]	gerade
to dial [ˈdaiəl]	wählen, drehen (Telefon)
to listen [lisn]	lauschen, zuhören
behind [biˈhaind]	hinter
three times	dreimal
engaged [inˈgeidʒd]	hier: besetzt
the fourth time	beim vierten Mal
to get through [θru:]	durchkommen
British Overseas Airways [ˈbritiʃ ˈəuvəsi:z ˈɛəweiz]	Britische Überseefluggesellschaft

flight [flait]	Flug
in the afternoon ['ɑ:ftə'nu:n]	*nachmittags*
April 2nd ['eipril ðə 'sekənd]	*lies: April the second*
to reserve [ri'zə:v]	reservieren
seat [si:t]	Platz
departure [di'pɑ:tʃə]	Abfahrt
arrival [ə'raivəl]	Ankunft
are there any stops on the way?	*gibt es unterwegs Zwischenlandungen?*
to travel back [trævl]	zurückreisen
return ticket [ri'tə:ntikit]	Rückflugkarte
to book [buk]	buchen, reservieren
double room ['dʌbl rum]	Doppelzimmer
fortnight ['fɔ:tnait]	zwei Wochen
to believe [bi'li:v]	glauben
to run away, ran, run [ʌ, æ, ʌ]	weglaufen
has he done anything wrong?	*hat er irgend etwas falsch gemacht?*
feeling ['fi:liŋ]	Gefühl
to learn [lə:n]	lernen
at school [sku:l]	in der Schule
to practise ['præktis]	ausüben, praktizieren
life, lives [laif, laivz]	Leben
instead [in'sted]	statt dessen
trouble [trʌbl]	Unannehmlichkeit, Sorge
date [deit]	Datum
to leave, left, left [li:v, e]	verlassen
three more weeks	drei weitere Wochen
birthday ['bə:θdei]	Geburtstag
cup [kʌp]	Tasse
saucer ['sɔ:sə]	Unterteller
envelope ['envələup]	Umschlag (Brief-)
football pools ['futbɔ:l 'pu:lz]	Fußballtoto

8. The Future

14 future ['fju:tʃə]	Zukunft
notice ['nəutis]	Ankündigung, Bekanntmachung
to stop	stehenbleiben
Paddington Station ['pædiŋtən 'steiʃən]	*Sackbahnhof in London*
to ring, rang, rung [i, æ, ʌ]	läuten
to follow ['fɔləu]	folgen
hall [hɔ:l]	Diele, Halle
would you like to sit down?	*möchten Sie sich setzen?*
to point to [pɔint]	weisen auf, zeigen auf
well	nun
left hand	linke Hand
to become, became, become [ʌ, ei, ʌ]	werden
great [greit]	groß, berühmt
daughter ['dɔ:tə]	Tochter
son [sʌn]	Sohn
plenty of ['plenti əv]	viel, eine Menge
to put, put, put [u]	setzen, stellen, legen
to worry ['wʌri]	sich Sorgen machen
to tell, told, told [e, əu]	sagen, erzählen
would you show me?	*würden Sie mir zeigen?*
you won't have to give me any money	*Sie brauchen mir kein Geld zu geben*
when I've finished ['finiʃt]	*wenn ich fertig bin*
I won't [wəunt]	ich werde nicht
I wouldn't be so sure [ʃuə]	*ich wäre nicht so sicher*
bright [brait]	hell, licht 15
game [geim]	Spiel

9. A Bet

bet	Wette
country ['kʌntri]	Land
Anglo-Saxon ['ængləu 'sæksən]	Angelsachse
Norman ['nɔ:mən]	Normanne
to conquer ['kɔnkə]	erobern
to speak, spoke, spoken [i:, əu, əu]	sprechen
language ['læŋgwidʒ]	Sprache
mixture ['mikstʃə]	Mischung
Germanic [dʒə'mænik]	germanisch
Dutch [dʌtʃ]	holländisch, Holländer

	Austrian ['ɔ:striən]	Österreicher
	to step	schreiten
	easy ['i:zi]	leicht
	may I? ['mei 'ai]	darf ich?
	together [tə'geðə]	zusammen
	guest [gest]	Gast
	menu ['menju:]	Speisekarte
	origin ['ɔridʒin]	Ursprung
	meal [mi:l]	Mahlzeit
16	Hyde Park ['haid 'pɑ:k]	*Park in London*
	table [teibl]	Tisch
	sir [sə:]	mein Herr (Anrede)
	would that be all right?	paßt der Ihnen?
	point [pɔint]	Punkt
	meat [mi:t]	Fleisch
	veal [vi:l]	Kalbfleisch
	beef [bi:f]	Rindfleisch
	mutton ['mʌtn]	Hammelfleisch
	beefsteak ['bi:f'steik]	Beefsteak
	vegetables, *Mehrz.* ['vedʒitəblz]	Gemüse
	pea [pi:]	Erbse
	bean [bi:n]	Bohne
	fruit [fru:t]	Frucht, Früchte
	cheese [tʃi:z]	Käse
	biscuits ['biskits]	Kekse
	a lot of	eine Menge, viel

10. Fast Cars

17	companion [kəm'pænjən]	Begleiterin
	invalid ['invəli:d]	kränklich, gebrechlich
	cinema ['sinəmə]	Kino
	dance [dɑ:ns]	Tanz
	to the seaside ['si:said]	an die See
	bus stop	Bushaltestelle
	the tennis international [intə'næʃənəl]	das internationale Tennisturnier
	they don't run very often	*sie verkehren nicht sehr häufig*
	get in	*steigen Sie ein*
	to accept [ək'sept]	annehmen
	glad [glæd]	froh
	foreigner ['fɔrinə]	Ausländer
	tall [tɔ:l]	groß
	suddenly ['sʌdnli]	plötzlich
	to remember [ri'membə]	sich erinnern
	prison [prizn]	Gefängnis
	to jump out of [dʒʌmp]	herausspringen aus
	traffic light ['træfik lait]	Verkehrsampel
	terrible ['teribl]	schrecklich
	miserable ['mizərəbl]	unglücklich, elend
	idea [ai'diə]	Idee
	fast [fɑ:st]	schnell
	shout [ʃaut]	Schrei, Ausruf
	pleasure ['pleʒə]	Freude, Vergnügen
	driving-mirror ['draiviŋ 'mirə]	Rückspiegel
	pig [pig]	Schwein
18	girl-friend ['gə:lfrend]	Freundin

11. A Second-hand Car

	second-hand car ['sekənd hænd 'kɑ:]	Gebrauchtwagen
	to sell, sold, sold [e, əu]	verkaufen
	to apply [ə'plai]	sich wenden an
	advertisement [əd'və:tismənt]	Anzeige, Annonce
	tube [tju:b]	Untergrundbahn, Röhre
	to knock [nɔk]	klopfen
	garage ['gærɑ:ʒ]	Garage
	to have a look at	*sich ansehen*
	practical ['præktikl]	praktisch
	that's all right	*ist schon gut*
	to send, sent, sent [e]	schicken
	to drive, drove, driven [draiv, drəuv, drivn]	fahren
	Marjorie ['mɑ:dʒəri]	*weibl. Vorname*
	we are going for a drive	*wir wollen eine Fahrt machen*
	beauty ['bju:ti]	Schönheit
	to belong to	jdm. gehören
	to press	drücken
	starter ['stɑ:tə]	Starter
	to put the car into bottom gear ['bɔtəm 'giə]	*den ersten Gang einlegen*
19	to speed, sped, sped [i:, e]	eilen, sausen, flitzen
	while the car was speeding along a narrow country road	*während der Wagen eine enge Landstraße entlangsauste*

speedometer [spi'dɔmitə]	Geschwindigkeitsmesser, Tachometer
needle ['ni:dl]	Nadel
to enjoy [in'dʒɔi]	genießen
to slow down ['sləu 'daun]	langsamer fahren
several times ['sevrəl]	mehrere Male
to try [trai]	versuchen
engine ['endʒin]	Motor
to climb out ['klaim 'aut]	herausklettern
to lift	heben
bonnet ['bɔnit]	Haube
to turn [tə:n]	drehen
screw [skru:]	Schraube
the engine would not start	*der Motor wollte nicht anspringen*
trick	Trick, Streich
wrong [rɔŋ]	falsch, nicht in Ordnung
worth [wə:θ]	wert
mechanic [mi'kænik]	Mechaniker
to glance at [glɑ:ns]	einen flüchtigen Blick werfen
petrol ['petrəl]	Benzin
gallon ['gælən]	Gallone (ca. 4,5 Liter)
empty ['emti]	leer
filling-station ['filiŋsteiʃən]	Tankstelle

12. The Superstitious Football Player

superstitious [sju:pə'stiʃəs]	abergläubisch
player ['pleiə]	Spieler
match [mætʃ]	Spiel, Wettkampf
bomber ['bɔmə]	Bomber
nobody ['nəubədi]	niemand
lucky charm [tʃɑ:m]	Glücksbringer, Talisman
neck	Hals
ladder ['lædə]	Leiter
to meet, met, met [i:, e]	treffen, kennenlernen
birth [bə:θ]	Geburt
versus, *lat.* ['və:səs]	gegen (beim Sport)
further on ['fə:ðər 'ɔn]	weiter
Wembley ['wembli]	*Fußballstadion in London*
in good time	*rechtzeitig*
dressing-room	Umkleideraum
to break, broke, broken [ei, əu]	zerbrechen
to pieces ['pi:siz]	*in Stücke*
to turn [tə:n]	hier: werden
sheet [ʃi:t]	Bettlaken
to think, thought, thought [θink, θɔ:t]	denken
spectator [spek'teitə]	Zuschauer 20
favourite ['feivrit]	Favorit
excitement ['ik'saitmənt]	Aufregung
goal [gəul]	Tor
to fall, fell, fallen [ɔ:, e, ɔ:]	fallen
everything went wrong	*alles ging schief*
they knew what the matter was	*sie wußten, was los war*
horseshoe ['hɔ:sʃu:]	Hufeisen
club manager ['klʌb 'mænidʒə]	Vereinsgeschäftsführer
unlucky charm [ʌn'lʌki 'tʃɑ:m]	böser Zauber
Kent	*südöstl. Grafschaft*
ready ['redi]	bereit
to hope [həup]	hoffen
as soon as	sobald als
wheel-chair ['wi:ltʃɛə]	Rollstuhl
since then	seitdem
for seven years	*sieben Jahre lang*
like	wie
conjuror ['kʌndʒərə]	Zauberer
pocket ['pɔkit]	Tasche (Kleider-)
peace [pi:s]	Friede
to keep one's form	*seine Form behalten* 21

13. A Race against Time

to wave [weiv]	winken, schwenken
to scream [skri:m]	schreien
hospital [ˈhɔspitl]	Krankenhaus
to poison [ˈpɔizn]	vergiften
to groan [grəun]	stöhnen
the back of the car	der Rücksitz des Wagens
to hurry [ˈhʌri]	sich beeilen
to live [liv]	leben
top speed [ˈtɔp ˈspi:d]	Höchstgeschwindigkeit
to happen [ˈhæpn]	geschehen, passieren
accident [ˈæksidənt]	Unglück
stranger [ˈstreindʒə]	Fremder, Unbekannter
to take s.o. to	jmd. hinbringen
pain [pein]	Schmerz
stomach [ˈstʌmək]	Magen
rain [rein]	Regen
to switch on	andrehen, einschalten
headlights [ˈhedlaits]	Scheinwerfer (am Auto)
quiet [kwaiət]	ruhig
distance [ˈdistəns]	Entfernung
light [lait]	Licht
to smoke [sməuk]	rauchen
22 thanks a lot	herzlichsten Dank
I'll manage it now	*ich schaffe es jetzt*
entrance [ˈentrəns]	Eingang
to disappear [disəˈpiə]	verschwinden
inside [ˈinˈsaid]	im Innern
to seem	scheinen
strange [streindʒ]	merkwürdig
to trust [trʌst]	trauen, glauben
to laugh [lɑ:f]	lachen
to slam [slæm]	zuschlagen (Tür)
to work [wə:k]	arbeiten
my car broke down	*mein Wagen hatte eine Panne*
tall story [tɔ:l ˈstɔ:ri]	tolle Geschichte, unglaubliche Geschichte
to join [dʒɔin]	(sich) anschließen
perhaps [pəˈhæps]	vielleicht
revenge [riˈvendʒ]	Rache

14. A New Life for Mrs Scott

serious [ˈsiəriəs]	ernstlich, ernsthaft
health [helθ]	Gesundheit
to visit [ˈvizit]	besuchen
trouble [ˈtrʌbl]	hier: Beschwerde, Leiden
physical [ˈfizikəl]	körperlich
mental [ˈmentəl]	seelisch, geistig
you ought to know best what the trouble is	*Sie müßten am besten wissen, was los ist*
marriage [ˈmæridʒ]	Heirat
to suffer [ˈsʌfə]	leiden
in silence [ˈsailəns]	schweigend
to change [ˈtʃeindʒ]	ändern
way of life	Lebensart
nonsense [ˈnɔnsəns]	Unsinn
upstairs [ˈʌpˈstɛəz]	nach oben 23
what kind of poison	welche Art Gift
weed-killer [ˈwi:dkilə]	Unkrautvertilgungsmittel
to murder [ˈmə:də]	umbringen, ermorden
dead [ded]	tot
at once	sofort
police inspector [pəˈlisinˈspektə]	Polizeikommissar
to question [ˈkwestʃən]	(be)fragen, verhören
I never did anything of the kind	*so etwas habe ich nie getan*
simply terrible [ˈsimpli ˈteribl]	einfach schrecklich
fly [flai]	Fliege
bottle [ˈbɔtl]	Flasche
quite [kwait]	ganz
cheerful [ˈtʃiəful]	fröhlich, gut gelaunt
downstairs [ˈdaunˈstɛəz]	unten, im Erdgeschoß
to exchange [iksˈtʃeindʒ]	austauschen
while [wail]	während
rich [ritʃ]	reich 24
will	Wille, Testament
in his favour [ˈfeivə]	zu seinen Gunsten
details [ˈdi:teilz]	Einzelheiten
theory [ˈθiəri]	Theorie
case [keis]	Fall
closed [kləuzd]	abgeschlossen

15. Two Strangers Meet

clerk [klɑ:k]	Angestellter
City ['siti]	*Geschäftsviertel von London*
to spend, spent, spent [e]	ausgeben
he could manage quite well ['mænidʒ]	*er kam ganz gut hin (mit dem Geld)*
suit [sju:t]	Anzug
to examine [ig'zæmin]	untersuchen
contents, *Mehrz.* ['kɔntents]	Inhalt
wallet ['wɔlit]	Brieftasche
to enjoy oneself	sich vergnügen
driver	Fahrer
box-office ['bɔksɔfis]	Kasse
house full	ausverkauft
air [ɛə]	hier: Miene, Aussehen
expert ['ekspə:t]	Fachmann, Experte
fur coat ['fə:'kəut]	Pelzmantel
to address s.o. [ə'dres]	anreden, sich wenden an jdn.
excuse me [iks'kju:z mi:]	entschuldigen Sie
worried ['wʌrid]	beunruhigt, verstimmt
may I ask you what the trouble is?	*darf ich fragen, was Sie bedrückt?*
harmless	harmlos
enough [i'nʌf]	genug
25 company ['kʌmpəni]	Gesellschaft
to introduce oneself [intrə'dju:s]	sich vorstellen
impressed [im'prest]	beeindruckt
to turn to	sich wenden an
companion [kəm'pænjən]	Begleiter(in)
what about dinner?	*wie wär's, wenn wir zu abend speisten?*
Prunier's [prun'jez]	*sehr teures Londoner Restaurant*
oyster ['ɔistə]	Auster
for myself	für mich
month [mʌnθ]	Monat
veal cutlet ['vi:l 'kʌtlit]	Kalbskotelett
chipped potatoes [tʃipt pə'teitəuz]	Pommes frites
basket ['bɑskit]	Korb
to amount to [ə'maunt]	sich belaufen auf
he thought better of it	*er besann sich eines Besseren*
bill	Rechnung
to order ['ɔ:də]	bestellen
to part [pɑ:t]	sich trennen
he couldn't bring himself to tell her the truth	*er brachte es nicht über sich, ihr die Wahrheit zu sagen*
to miss	versäumen, verpassen
straight [streit]	geradewegs, direkt
to make a fool of oneself [fu:l]	*sich lächerlich machen*
to pretend [pri'tend]	vorgeben, behaupten

16. Journey's End

journey [dʒə:ni]	Reise 26
district ['distrikt]	Bezirk, Viertel
to shut, shut, shut [ʌ]	schließen
to move on ['mu:v‿ɔn]	sich vorwärts bewegen, weitergehen
doorway ['dɔ:wei]	Türeingang, Einfahrt
to walk up to s.o.	*zu jdm. hingehen*
it's all right, officer	*'s ist schon recht, Wachtmeister*
appointment [ə'pɔintmənt]	Verabredung
twenty years ago [ə'gəu]	vor zwanzig Jahren
to explain to s.o. [iks'plein]	jdm. etwas erklären
pub [pʌb]	Gastwirtschaft
building ['bildiŋ]	Gebäude
in its place	*an die Stelle*
match [mætʃ]	Streichholz
about, *Adv.*	ungefähr
lip	Lippe
to sail to	das Schiff nehmen nach
in the world [wə:ld]	*auf der Welt*
to be alive [ə'laiv]	lebendig, am Leben sein
coat [kəut]	Mantel
opposite ['ɔpəzit]	entgegengesetzt
sure enough ['ʃuər‿i'nʌf]	hier: wahrhaftig 27

never mind ['nevə 'maind]	*macht nichts*
States [steits]	Staaten (USA)
bad character ['kæriktə]	schlechter Charakter
to be wanted	gesucht werden
police station [pə'li:s 'steiʃən]	Polizeirevier
appointed place [ə'pɔintid 'pleis]	verabredeter Ort
to light [lait]	anzünden
plain clothes man ['plein kləuðz 'mæn]	Polizist in Zivil

17. Queen Victoria

Victoria [vik'tɔ:riə]	*Königin v. England v. 1837–1901*
prince [prins]	Prinz
to be the same age [eidʒ]	*gleich alt sein*
real ['riəl]	wirklich
democracy [di'mɔkrəsi]	Demokratie
to exist [ig'zist]	bestehen, vorhanden sein
coronation [kɔrə'neiʃən]	Krönung
the poor ['puə]	die Armen
whose [hu:z]	deren
factory ['fæktəri]	Fabrik
to die [dai]	sterben
to change for the better	*sich zum Besseren wenden*
in the social field ['səuʃəl]	auf sozialem Gebiet
to rule [ru:l]	herrschen über, beherrschen
empire ['empaiə]	Imperium, Reich
Empress of India ['empris‿əv‿'indjə]	Kaiserin von Indien
magnificent [mæg'nifisənt]	großartig
ceremony ['seriməni]	Zeremonie, Feierlichkeit
for a long time	hier: seit langem
height [hait]	Höhe, Höhepunkt
power ['pauə]	Macht
28 constitutional [kɔnsti'tju:ʃənl]	verfassungsmäßig
duty ['dju:ti]	Pflicht
to fulfil [ful'fil]	erfüllen
mass [mæs]	Masse
document ['dɔkjumənt]	Dokument
to deal with, dealt, dealt [di:l, e]	sich beschäftigen mit
busy [bizi]	geschäftig
time-table ['taimteibl]	Fahrplan, Stundenplan, Zeitplan
to observe [əb'zə:v]	beachten, beobachten, einhalten
to the minute ['minit]	auf die Minute
though [ðəu]	obgleich
to love [lʌv]	lieben
quarrel ['kwɔrəl]	Streit
proud [praud]	stolz
sometimes ['sʌmtaimz]	manchmal
sovereign ['sɔvrin]	Herrscher(in)
private ['praivit]	privat
the Houses of Parliament ['hauziz‿əv 'pɑ:ləmənt]	Parlamentsgebäude in London
the way she ordered him about	die Art, wie sie ihn herumkommandierte
key [ki:]	Schlüssel
behaviour [bi'heivjə]	Benehmen, Verhalten
impossible [im'pɔsibl]	unmöglich
to repeat [ri'pi:t]	wiederholen
beetroot ['bi:tru:t]	rote Beete
finally ['fainəli]	schließlich
different ['difrənt]	andersartig, anderer
shy [ʃai]	scheu, schüchtern

18. A Worker's Family at the Time of Queen Victoria

worker ['wə:kə]	Arbeiter
Manchester ['mæntʃistə]	*Stadt im NW Englands*
to attend s.o. [ə'tend]	besuchen, pflegen, behandeln
fitter	Monteur
packer ['pækə]	Packer(in)
tired ['taiəd]	müde
to earn [ə:n]	verdienen 29
brickfield ['brikfi:ld]	Ziegelei
to carry ['kæri]	tragen
heavy ['hevi]	schwer
brick	Ziegel, Backstein

wages, *Mehrz.* ['weidʒiz]	Lohn
chimney-sweep ['tʃimniswi:p]	Kaminfeger
to lose, lost, lost [lu:z, ɔ]	verlieren
to be employed [im'plɔid]	beschäftigt sein
parents ['pɛərənts]	Eltern
rather a small girl ['rɑ:ðə]	*ein ziemlich kleines Mädchen*
to creep, crept, crept [kri:p, krept]	kriechen
machine [mə'ʃi:n]	Maschine
to clean [kli:n]	säubern, reinigen
children were not allowed [ə'laud]	*Kinder durften nicht*
matchbox	Streichholzschachtel
2½d. ['tʌpəns 'heipni]	2½ pennies, etwa 8 Pf
ever ['evə]	jemals
outside Manchester	außerhalb von Manchester
illness ['ilnis]	Krankheit
unemployment ['ʌnim'plɔimənt]	Arbeitslosigkeit
workhouse ['wə:khaus]	Armenhaus, in dem man arbeiten mußte
to fear [fiə]	fürchten
worse than death ['wə:s ðən 'deθ]	schlimmer als der Tod

19. Noise in the Night

Appleton ['æpltən]	*engl. Familienname*
country house ['kʌntrihaus]	Landhaus
card-playing ['kɑ:dpleiiŋ]	Kartenspiel
party game ['pɑ:tigeim]	Gesellschaftsspiel
laughter ['lɑ:ftə]	Lachen
Christmas Eve ['krisməs'i:v]	Weihnachtsabend
to decorate ['dekəreit]	schmücken
balloon [bə'lu:n]	Ballon
holly ['hɔli]	Stechpalme
mistletoe ['misltəu]	Mistelzweig
Marilyn ['mærilin]	*weibl. Vorname*
cousin [kʌzn]	Vetter, Base
entertaining [entə'teiniŋ]	unterhaltend
loud [laud]	laut
important [im'pɔ:tənt]	wichtig, gewichtig
snoring ['snɔ:riŋ]	Schnarchen
alarm clock [ə'lɑ:m klɔk]	Wecker
to rise, rose, risen [raiz, rəuz, rizn]	aufstehen
news [nju:z]	Nachricht 30
sleepless ['sli:plis]	schlaflos
sleeping-tablet ['sli:piŋ tæblit]	Schlaftablette
louder than ever	lauter denn je
to hang, hung, hung [æ, ʌ]	hängen
crematorium [kremə'tɔ:riəm]	Krematorium
sorry for the trouble	Entschuldigung für die Umstände
message ['mesidʒ]	Botschaft, Mitteilung
paper-bag ['peipə bæg]	Papiertüte
air [ɛə]	Luft
staircase wall ['stɛəkeis 'wɔ:l]	Treppenwand
to howl [haul]	heulen
to discover [dis'kʌvə]	entdecken
gun [gʌn]	Schußwaffe
to awake, awoke, awoke [ə'weik, ə'wəuk]	wecken, aufwachen
joke [dʒəuk]	Scherz

20. English Habits

habit ['hæbit]	Gewohnheit
Appleby ['æplbi]	*engl. Familienname*
kitchen ['kitʃin]	Küche
to peel [pi:l]	schälen
to cook [kuk]	kochen 31
to be surrounded by [sə'raundid]	umgeben sein von
stamp [stæmp]	Briefmarke
Tom, Dick or Harry	*Hinz und Kunz*
reason ['ri:zn]	Grund
custom ['kʌstəm]	Sitte
mantelpiece ['mæntlpi:s]	Kaminsims
to call [kɔ:l]	zu Besuch kommen
effort ['efət]	Anstrengung

Red Lion ['red 'laiən]	Roter Löwe
round [raund]	Runde
beer [biə]	Bier
closing time ['kləuziŋ taim]	Polizeistunde
queue [kju:]	Schlange (v. Menschen)
if you don't mind	*wenn Sie nichts dagegen haben*
32 careful [kɛəful]	vorsichtig
page [peidʒ]	Seite
to cover up ['kʌvər‿'ʌp]	bedecken
comfortable ['kʌmfətəbl]	bequem

21. A Visit to Stratford-on-Avon

visit ['vizit]	Besuch
Stratford-on-Avon ['strætfəd‿ɔn‿'eivn]	*Geburtsort Shakespeares*
Birmingham ['bə:miŋəm]	*große engl. Industriestadt*
dining-car ['dainiŋ kɑ:]	Speisewagen
Leamington Spa ['lemiŋtən 'spɑ:]	*Badeort in Mittelengland*
pleasant ['pleznt]	angenehm, freundlich
market town ['mɑ:kit 'taun]	Kleinstadt
half-timbered house ['hɑ:ftimbəd 'haus]	Fachwerkhaus
to date from [deit]	stammen aus (einer Zeit)
Shakespeare ['ʃeikspiə]	*engl. Dichter (1564–1616)*
grammar school ['græməsku:l]	höhere Schule
Latin ['lætin]	Latein
less	weniger
Greek [gri:k]	Griechisch
New Place	*Name eines Hauses*
poet ['pəuit]	Dichter
Royal Theatre ['θiətə]	*Königl. Theater*
performance [pə'fɔ:məns]	Vorstellung
in advance ['in‿əd'vɑ:ns]	im voraus
to lie, lay, lain [lai, lei, lein]	liegen
River Avon ['rivər‿'eivn]	*Name eines Flusses*
sun [sʌn]	Sonne
to shine, shone, shone [ʃain, ʃɔn]	scheinen
meadow ['medəu]	Wiese
gallery ['gæləri]	Galerie
stage [steidʒ]	Bühne
to understand, understood, understood [ʌndə'stænd, ʌndə'stud]	verstehen
to read, read, read [ri:d, red, red]	lesen
I managed to follow	ich konnte folgen
Holy Trinity Church ['həuli 'triniti 'tʃə:tʃ]	Heilige Dreifaltigkeitskirche
tombstone ['tu:mstəun]	Grabstein
to rest [rest]	ruhen
grave [greiv]	Grab 33
to write, wrote, written [rait, rəut, ritn]	schreiben
written by himself	von ihm selbst geschrieben
dust [dʌst]	Staub
his dust should be left in peace	*sein Staub sollte in Frieden gelassen werden*
line [lain]	Zeile
blessed ['blesid]	gesegnet
to spare [spɛə]	verschonen, übrig haben
stone [stəun]	Stein
cursed ['kə:sid]	verflucht
bones [bəunz]	Gebeine, Knochen
age [eidʒ]	Alter, Zeitalter

22. A Performance at the Stratford Royal Theatre

As You Like It	Wie Es Euch Gefällt
central figure	Hauptfigur
comedy ['kɔmidi]	Komödie
female character ['fi:meil]	hier: Frauengestalt
love story ['lʌvstɔ:ri]	Liebesgeschichte
serious character ['siəriəs]	hier: ernster Inhalt
merely ['miəli]	lediglich, bloß
part [pɑ:t]	Rolle
to cry [krai]	weinen, schreien
nurse [nə:s]	Amme
satchel ['sætʃəl]	Ranzen, Schultasche

unwillingly [ʌn'wiliŋli]	unwillig
lover [lʌvə]	Liebhaber
to sing, sang, sung [i, æ, ʌ]	singen
love-song	Liebeslied
darling girl	Liebchen
soldier ['səuldʒə]	Soldat
fame [feim]	Ruhm
advice, *Einz.* [əd'vais]	Rat, Ratschläge
trousers, *Mehrz.* ['trauzəz]	Hose
leg [leg]	Bein
manly ['mænli]	männlich
voice [vɔis]	Stimme
scene [si:n]	Szene
childhood ['tʃaildhud]	Kindheit
tooth, teeth [tu:θ, ti:θ]	Zahn, Zähne
taste [teist]	Geschmack
34 excursion [iks'kə:ʃən]	Ausflug
joy [dʒɔi]	Freude
for ever	für immer

23. Good-bye, Charlie!

Cup Final ['kʌp 'fainəl]	Pokalendspiel
crowd [kraud]	Menschenmenge
military band ['militəri 'bænd]	Militärkapelle
lawn [lɔ:n]	Rasen
to shake, shook, shaken [ei, u, ei]	schütteln
team [ti:m]	Mannschaft
Luton Town ['lu:tən 'taun]	*engl. Fußballmannschaft*
Nottingham Forest ['nɔtiŋəm 'fɔrist]	*engl. Fußballmannschaft*
fight [fait]	Kampf
to succeed in [sək'si:d]	gelingen zu
net	Netz
to receive [ri'si:v]	empfangen, erhalten
on board [bɔ:d]	an Bord
weather ['weðə]	Wetter
wet	naß
and yet	und doch
by coach [kəutʃ]	mit Autobussen
on foot [fut]	zu Fuß
platform ['plætfɔ:m]	Bahnsteig
station square [skwɛə]	Bahnhofsplatz
sardine [sɑ:'di:n]	Sardine
tin	Dose, Büchse
church bell ['tʃə:tʃ bel]	Kirchenglocke
danger ['deindʒə]	Gefahr
to trample ['træmpl]	trampeln
to pull off [pul]	wegreißen
body ['bɔdi]	Körper
fortunately ['fɔ:tʃnitli]	glücklicherweise
offer ['ɔfə]	Angebot 35
to offer ['ɔfə]	anbieten
sum [sʌm]	Summe
I don't mind telling you	*ich will dir offen sagen*
to object to [əb'dʒekt]	etwas dagegen haben, Einwände haben
opportunity [ɔpə'tju:niti]	Gelegenheit
both for you and for the club [bəuθ]	*sowohl für dich als auch für den Club*
slave [sleiv]	Sklave
that's different	*das ist etwas anderes*
case [keis]	Fall
to expect [iks'pekt]	erwarten

24. Teaching by Telephone

teaching by telephone ['ti:tʃiŋ bai 'telifəun]	Unterricht per Telephon 36
foreign ['fɔrin]	ausländisch, fremd
Ltd = Limited ['limitid]	Gesellschaft mit beschränkter Haftung (GmbH)
Wolverhampton ['wulvə'hæmtən]	*Industriestadt in Mittelengland*
your ref. (= reference) ['refrəns]	Ihr Zeichen (Bezug)
Wheatley ['wi:tli]	*Familienname*
Tree Tops ['tri: tɔps]	Baumwipfel *(Name eines Hauses)*
Codsall ['kɔdsɔ:l]	*Ort i. d. Nähe v. Wolverhampton*
to correspond ['kɔris'pɔnd]	korrespondieren
quite a number	eine ganze Anzahl
method ['meθəd]	Methode
to prove [pru:v]	sich erweisen

successful [sək'sesful]	erfolgreich
member ['membə]	Mitglied
staff [stɑ:f]	Personal
tyre factory ['taiə 'fæktəri]	Reifenfabrik
to wonder ['wʌndə]	sich fragen
whether ['weðə]	ob
to take on, took, taken [ei, u, ei]	auf sich nehmen, übernehmen
job [dʒɔb]	Aufgabe, Arbeit, Stelle
we have pleasure	*wir gestatten uns*
to enclose [in'kləuz]	beifügen
to suggest [sə'dʒest]	vorschlagen
to last [lɑ:st]	dauern
each [i:tʃ]	jeder
to book	buchen, belegen
course [kɔ:s]	Kursus
fee [fi:]	Honorar, Gebühr
£1.90 (one pound, ninety pence)	*ca. 16,50 DM*
grateful ['greitful]	dankbar
possible ['pɔsibl]	möglich
undertake, -took, -taken [ʌndə'teik, -'tuk, -'teikn]	unternehmen, übernehmen
Yours sincerely ['jɔ:z sin'siəli]	*hochachtungsvoll!*
37 J. M. C. Taylor, Esq. (= Esquire) [is'kwaiə] = Mr J. M. C. Taylor	*nur in Anschriften verwendete Bezeichnung für Herr*
23rd inst. (= instant) ['instənt]	23. d. M. (= dieses Monats)
to be prepared [pri'pɛəd]	bereit sein

tasty ['teisti]	schmackhaft
to be surprised [sə'praizd]	überrascht sein
to announce [ə'nauns]	ankündigen
to push [puʃ]	schieben, drücken
nose [nəuz]	Nase
price [prais]	Preis 38
tinned sausages ['sɔsidʒiz]	Würste in Dosen
managing director ['mænidʒiŋ di'rektə]	leitender Direktor
worth [wə:θ]	wert
somebody else	jemand anderes
I mean it	*ich meine es wirklich*
desk	Schreibtisch, Pult
any time	jederzeit, irgendwann
kind regards to [ri'gɑ:dz]	*Empfehlung an*
bye [bai]	tschüs
to hang up, hung, hung [æ, ʌ]	hier: Hörer auflegen
on advertising ['ædvətaiziŋ]	*für Werbung*
expenses [iks'pensiz]	Auslagen, Spesen
net income ['net'inkʌm]	Nettoeinkommen
to believe [bi'li:v]	glauben
especially [is'peʃəli]	besonders
to mix	mischen
to declare [di'klɛə]	angeben
tax office ['tæks‿ɔfis]	Finanzamt
tax inspector ['tæks‿in'spektə]	Steuerbeamter 39
inquiry [in'kwaiəri]	Frage, Nachforschung
income-tax return ['inkəmtæks ri'tə:n]	Einkommensteuererklärung

25. A Man Called Smith

called	namens, genannt
father-in-law ['fɑ:ðərin'lɔ:]	Schwiegervater
to prepare [pri'pɛə]	vorbereiten
event [i'vent]	Ereignis
on the phone [fəun]	am Telefon
receiver [ri'si:və]	Hörer (d. Telefons)
to pay a visit	besuchen
secretary ['sekrətri]	Sekretär(in)
cigar [si'gɑ:]	Zigarre

26. London

huge [hju:dʒ]	riesig
Ireland ['aiələnd]	Irland
Wales [weilz]	Wales
one-way train	Zug ohne Wiederkehr
capital ['kæpitl]	Hauptstadt
to pick up	aufheben
wealthy ['welθi]	wohlhabend
true	wahr, hier: es stimmt

same [seim]	gleich
profession [prə'feʃən]	Beruf
than anywhere else	*als sonstwo*
cost of living	Lebenshaltungskosten
he is to be at his office	*er soll im Büro sein*
Caterham, Surrey ['keitərəm, 'sʌri]	*Ort in der Grafschaft Surrey, südl. von London*
commuter [kə'mju:tə]	Pendler
suburb ['sʌbə:b]	Vorort
they will lunch	sie essen gewöhnlich zu Mittag
canteen [kæn'ti:n]	Kantine
official [ə'fiʃəl]	amtlich, offiziell
report [ri'pɔ:t]	Bericht
per cent [pə'sent]	Prozent
Second World War ['sekənd 'wə:ld 'wɔ:]	2. Weltkrieg
warehouse ['wɛəhaus]	Lagerhaus, Kaufhaus
blitz	Bombenangriff auf England im 2. Weltkrieg
to go up in the air	*in die Luft fliegen*
left	übrig(gelassen)
to sweep, swept, swept [i:, e]	fegen
St. Paul's Cathedral [snt'pɔ:lz kə'θidrəl]	St.-Pauls-Kathedrale
completely [kəm'pli:tli]	vollständig
40 to draw, drew, drawn [ɔ:, u:, ɔ:]	ziehen
population [pɔpju'leiʃən]	Bevölkerung
the dream will never come true	*der Traum wird nie Wirklichkeit werden*

27. A Letter from America

inhabitant [in'hæbitənt]	Einwohner
Empire State Building	*ca. 449 m hoch*
Chicago [ʃi'kɑ:gəu]	*ca. 3,7 Mill. Einw.*
Pentagon, the USA Department of Defence [di'fens]	Pentagon, das amerikan. Verteidigungsministerium
Grand Central Terminal ['tə:minəl]	*Hauptbahnhof in New York*
etc. [it'setrə]	usw.
cult [kʌlt]	Kult
to be looked upon as	betrachtet werden als
special ['speʃəl]	besonderer
craze [kreiz]	Narrheit, Fimmel
cemetery ['semitri]	Friedhof
to be taken care of	gepflegt werden
bulldog ['buldɔg]	Bulldogge
national ['næʃənəl]	national
symbol ['simbəl]	Symbol
even ['i:vən]	sogar
crazy about [kreizi]	verrückt auf
to agree [ə'gri:]	zustimmen
we British	wir Briten
statistics, *Mehrz.* [stə'tistiks]	Statistik
twice [twais]	zweimal
title ['taitl]	Titel
human ['hjumən]	menschlich
to be blue-blooded ['blu:'blʌdid]	blaues Blut haben, reinrassig sein
dog sitter ['dɔgsitə]	jemand, der Hunde beaufsichtigt
dog walker ['dɔgwɔ:kə]	jemand, der Hunde ausführt
pet	Lieblingstier, Schoßhund
every quarter of any town ['kwɔ:tə]	jedes Viertel jeder beliebigen Stadt
trade [treid]	Handel 41
non-stop ['nɔn'stɔp]	durchgehend
amount of space [ə'maunt‿əv 'speis]	Raumanteil
supermarket ['sju:pə'mɑ:kit]	Supermarkt
to prefer [pri'fə:]	vorziehen
Great Dane ['greit 'dein]	deutsche Dogge
St. Bernard [snt 'bə:nəd]	Bernhardiner
Old English Sheepdog ['ʃi:pdɔg]	*bes. große engl. Hunderasse*
it's no use [its 'nəu 'ju:s]	*es nützt nichts*
dachshund ['dækshund]	Dachshund, Dackel

28. Compromise throughout the Centuries

compromise throughout the centuries ['kɔmprəmaiz θru'aut ðə 'sentʃuriz]	Kompromiß durch die Jahrhunderte
talent ['tælənt]	Talent
characteristic [kæriktə'ristik]	typische Eigenschaft
to form	bilden
historic [his'tɔrik]	historisch
to come into being	*entstehen*
assembly [ə'sembli]	Versammlung
baron ['bærən]	Baron
knight [nait]	Ritter
citizen ['sitizn]	Bürger
unless [ən'les]	es sei denn
situation [sitju'eiʃən]	Situation, Lage
to support [sə'pɔ:t]	unterstützen
angry ['æŋgri]	böse, ungehalten
eventually [i'ventʃuəli]	mit der Zeit, schließlich
to retire [ri'taiə]	sich zurückziehen
wing	Flügel
Westminster Palace ['westminstə 'pælis]	Westminster Palast, *urspr. kgl. Palast, heute Parlamentsgebäude*
to debate [di'beit]	debattieren, beraten
to agree [ə'gri:]	sich einig werden, zustimmen
Speaker ['spi:kə]	Sprecher
two-chamber system ['tu:'tʃeimbə sistim]	Zwei-Kammern-System
House of Lords ['haus‿əv 'lɔ:dz]	Oberhaus
House of Commons ['haus‿əv 'kɔmənz]	Unterhaus
desired [di'zaiəd]	begehrt
position [pə'ziʃən]	Position, Posten
nevertheless ['nevəðə'les]	nichtsdestoweniger
to elect [i'lekt]	wählen
to refuse [ri'fju:z]	ablehnen
to push [puʃ]	stoßen
to be executed ['eksikju:tid]	hingerichtet werden
composed [kəm'pəuzd]	zusammengesetzt 42
landed gentry ['lændid 'dʒentri]	niederer Landadel
townspeople ['taunzpi:pl]	Städter, Stadtbewohner
group [gru:p]	Gruppe
to differ ['difə]	sich unterscheiden
to survive [sə'vaiv]	überleben
in the face of	angesichts
to get accustomed to [ə'kʌstəmd]	sich gewöhnen an
connection [kə'nekʃən]	Verbindung
to inherit [in'herit]	erben
property ['prɔpəti]	Besitz
ordinary ['ɔ:dinəri]	gewöhnlich
clear [kliə]	klar
rare [rɛə]	selten
French Revolution [revə'lu:ʃən]	*Französische Revolution v. 1789*
cruelty ['kruəlti]	Grausamkeit
link	Verbindung, Band
to connect [kə'nekt]	verbinden
to decrease [di'kri:s]	abnehmen
political [pə'litikəl]	politisch
career [kə'riə]	Laufbahn, Karriere
elderly ['eldəli]	ältere(r)
statesman ['steitsmən]	Staatsmann
to honour ['ɔnə]	ehren
former ['fɔ:mə]	früherer
milkman ['milkmən]	Milchmann
chairman ['tʃɛəmən]	Vorsitzender
Labour Party ['leibə 'pɑ:ti]	*engl. Arbeiterpartei*
Lambeth ['læmbəθ]	*Ortsteil von London*
example [ig'zɑ:mpl]	Beispiel
course [kɔ:s]	Lauf
monarchy ['mɔnəki]	Monarchie
however [hau'evə]	jedoch
to abolish [ə'bɔliʃ]	abschaffen
European [juərə'pi:ən]	europäisch
absolute ['æbsəlu:t]	absolut
representative [repri'zentətiv]	Vertreter
people	Volk, Leute
to solve [sɔlv]	lösen
Empire problem ['prɔbləm]	Problem des brit. Weltreichs
colony ['kɔləni]	Kolonie
Algeria [æl'dʒiəriə]	Algerien

to oblige [ə'blaidʒ]	zwingen, verpflichten
to remain [ri'mein]	bleiben, verbleiben
Commonwealth ['kɔmənwelθ]	*Völkergemeinschaft ehem. brit. Kolonien mit dem Mutterland*
to observe [əb'zə:v]	beachten
rule [ru:l]	Regel
history ['histəri]	Geschichte
to suffer ['sʌfə]	(er)leiden
set-back ['setbæk]	Rückschlag
loss	Verlust
to teach, taught, taught [ti:tʃ, tɔ:t]	lehren
this taught the English a lesson	*dies erteilte den Engländern eine Lektion*
sign [sain]	Zeichen

43

unrest ['ʌn'rest]	Unruhe
to grant [grɑ:nt]	gewähren
home rule ['həum'ru:l]	Selbstverwaltung, Autonomie
vast [vɑ:st]	weit, ausgedehnt
attitude ['ætitju:d]	Haltung
to save [seiv]	ersparen, bewahren vor
development [di'veləpmənt]	Entwicklung
gift	Gabe